Praise for *Dispatches from Bitter America*

A self-proclaimed gun-toting, chicken-eating son-of-a-Baptist, Todd Starnes uses Southern sensibilities mixed with homespun humor to take us along his journey across America. In *Dispatches from Bitter America* this "Great American" finds that not only is our American way of life under attack, but also that most Americans do in fact love God, this country, their families and are anything but bitter!

> —Sean Hannity, *New York Times* best-selling author, host of the syndicated *Sean Hannity* radio show and FOX News' *Hannity*

Todd Starnes is a masterful storyteller. In *Dispatches from Bitter America*, he offers commentary on today's current events through the lens of a self-proclaimed gun-toting, fried-chicken-eating son of a Baptist. Todd has always been one of my favorite news personalities and good friends. Now he is one of my favorite storytellers. Warning: don't start reading this book unless you are prepared to finish it. It's just that good.

> —Thom S. Rainer, President and CEO, LifeWay Christian Resources

In the great tradition of Mark Twain's classic essays, Starnes's *Dispatches* are alternately filled with belly laughs and bellicose observations, riveting stories and troubling revelations, as well as patriotic pleas and everyman advice. *Dispatches* is a free-wheeling blend of journalism and editorial opinion, with an added shot of satire blended into the mix.

> —Dr. Gene Fant, a dean and English professor, Union University

Todd Starnes's newest book, *Dispatches from Bitter America*, is everything I thought it would be. Todd uses his classic biting humor and sarcasm to drive home his points. He is merciless when writing about the insane and irrational decisions being made in America today. He may make you uncomfortable, but what he says is true. *This book is the antithesis of political correctness, which is why I couldn't put it down.* Every page is a reminder that we are losing touch and the favor of God in the land that we all love.

> —Michael Catt, senior pastor, Sherwood Church, Albany, Georgia, executive producer, Sherwood Pictures

Todd Starnes combines sound research with his signature wit to tell the stories of regular Americans who are standing up to a secular movement that seeks to remove all religious expression from the public square. This is a compelling book that puts our entire existence into the perspective of eternity.

—Tony Perkins, president, Family Research Council

Todd Starnes knows how to take any story and make me want to listen on FOX News. *Dispatches from Bitter America* shows that Todd can also write from the heart and make me want to read more! Classic Starnes!

—Matt Patrick, morning talk-show host,
News/Talk 740 KTRH, Houston, Texas

In the spirit of getting better—not bitter—Todd's *Dispatches from Bitter America* is a masterpiece that appeals from the boardroom to the trash truck in it's humorous appeal to our good sense. He takes us on a wild ride across America, snagging blue collar workers right along with corporate CEOs, to ask, "What is this world coming to?" A journalist with an eye for detail, his words had me laughing out loud in places I shouldn't have, while praying earnestly for the ridiculously desperate corner we have gotten ourselves into as Americans and as evangelical Christians.

—Joni B. Hannigan, managing editor,
Florida Baptist Witness

Todd Starnes captures the sentiments many Americans feel as they helplessly watch the traditional values they grew up with being stomped out and overruled by political correctness. Todd's stories will strike a chord, whether it's "The War on Christmas," "Tag—You're Out," or "The Chocolate Czar." Brownies now banned from school? Bah hum-bug.

—Gretchen Carlson, cohost of *Fox and Friends*

Dispatches from Bitter America features Todd Starnes at his best. With his trademark wit, Todd tackles questions being asked by Americans who wonder what is happening to our country.

Todd manages to get to the heart of the matter in a way that is both packed with information and sprinkled with humor. He is a man of immense faith, madly in love with our country, and endowed by his creator with the unique talent to tell a story like very few can. *Dispatches from Bitter America* is the best book I've read this year.

—Jeff Katz, morning host, Talk Radio 12000, Boston

DISPATCHES FROM
BITTER
AMERICA

TODD STARNES

B&H
PUBLISHING GROUP

Nashville, Tennessee

ISBN: 978-1-4336-7275-0

Published by B&H Publishing Group
Nashville, Tennessee

Dewey Decimal Classification: 361.6
Subject Heading: SOCIAL POLICY \ UNITED STATES—
CIVILIZATION \ CULTURE CONFLICT

1 2 3 4 5 6 7 8 9 • 16 15 14 13 12

This book is dedicated to:

Uncle Jerry—the original gun-toting Bitter American

In Memory of:

Great Uncle Bunny—a decorated veteran of WWII

Acknowledgments

First and foremost, I give glory to the Author of my salvation—my Lord and Savior, Jesus Christ. He gave me life everlasting and is my constant companion on this never-ending journey.

I'm especially thankful to my wonderful family. They keep me laughing and thinking year-round. I'm blessed with a great family tree. A special thank you to Aunt Lynn, Aunt Norma, Amy, Kristina, Saundra, and Bill. Oh, Bill. You've walked alongside me through two books now. And I'm a better writer because of you. It has been an epic journey, cousin. I owe you a pound of chocolate.

To my researchers, Cory, Cousin Daniel, and Garrett, I know the work was tedious, but you did such an amazing job. Garrett, thanks for your snarkiness—and your refreshing take on pop culture. Cory, thank you for taking time in between baseball games to field questions about politics! You hit a home run. Daniel, you are simply brilliant.

The team at B&H is tremendously spectacular. Julie, you had me at the blueberry cobbler. Selma, Kim, Lawrence, John, and Gary—you've been such a blessing to work with. And what can I say about the wonderful sales team? Thank you!

I'm also blessed to have one of the finest literary agents in the business. Frank Breeden, thank you for your wisdom, your guidance and your encouragement. And my legal team—Bryce and Kristen—mega-thanks!

Great friends are a precious source of encouragement and I'm grateful for many who helped me through the writing of this book—Elise, Sarah, Kellen, Blake, Derek, Lauren, Tara, Jessica, Willie, Shannon, Kevin, Paul, Robyn, and Tonya.

To my dear friend Kenton, you've taught me to appreciate the more refined way of New York City living—but I'm still not going to wear a bow tie. You are a dear brother in the Lord.

Finally, a special thank you to my readers and listeners. Some of the finest radio stations in the nation are carrying my daily commentaries. Thank you! And I can't begin to thank my readers: your letters, e-mail, and tweets have brought joy to my life and a smile to my face.

You are the kind of people who make this country the greatest on the planet.

Bitter Americans? Hardly.

Blessed Americans? Absolutely.

Contents

Dispatches from the Schoolhouse

Dispatches from the Pew

Introduction

I am a gun-toting, chicken-eating son of a Baptist. And according to the president of the United States, I am a bitter American.

President Obama delivered the diagnosis for my condition during the 2008 presidential campaign. In one of his rare, unscripted moments, then Senator Obama vented to a group of supporters in San Francisco about white, working-class voters.

"So it's not surprising then that they get bitter. They cling to guns or religion or antipathy to people who aren't like them or anti-immigrant sentiment or anti-trade sentiment as a way to explain their frustrations,"[1] he said, according to a transcript on *The Huffington Post*.

What a relief! I can pack away the antacid tablets. I always thought that bitter feeling in my belly was an upset stomach. But I don't have acid indigestion. I'm just a bitter American. I can't begin to tell you how indebted I am to the president of the United States for diagnosing my condition.

The antithesis of bitter Americans, I imagine, would be our countrymen who've been educated in Ivy League schools, who listen to highbrow music, and who dine on arugula and fermented soy. They are well-bred men who marry high-society women named Babs and Muffy. They are Americans who believe the only free speech should be their own. They are Americans who would rather the criminals have guns than law-abiding citizens. And they are Americans who believe mankind created the heavens and the earth and that man created God in his likeness.

But I do wonder about my prognosis for recovery. Will I have to turn my guns over to the federal government? Will I need to repent for the mass slaughter of innocent chickens to satisfy my bloodlust for finger-licking good food? Will I need to renounce my faith in the King of kings and instead bow my knee to whoever Oprah Winfrey ordains as "The One"?

Kind readers, these are lofty questions far above my pickup truck-driving, country music-listening, Paula Deen-loving pedigree. So I decided to hit the road in search of answers. What does it mean to be a bitter American? Is there a cure? And if so, do I want to take the medicine?

My search for answers took me through the cornfields of Iowa and the waters of South Carolina's low country; I traversed the Mississippi Delta and braved the scorching heat of the Nevada deserts. I was nearly mugged in Detroit and caught flu in Chicago, but I pressed on toward the prize. And one day it suddenly hit me. I was somewhere between a red state and a blue state when I had something of a political epiphany.

It happened at a small diner tucked away on a side street in the picturesque town of Manchester, New Hampshire. The Red Arrow Diner has been serving up blue-plate specials on Lowell Street since 1922. And it's also become a mandatory stop on the campaign trail for anyone who wants to take up residence at 1600 Pennsylvania Avenue.

It was a cold, snowy day, just before the New Hampshire primary. I peeled off my winter coat and grabbed the first stool I could find. The waitress told me they made the best cheeseburger in town so that's what I ordered—along with a root beer.

As I was waiting for my meal, I thought about my epiphany. The network television reporters like to tell us we are a divided people—that most Americans don't buy into God and country. But that's not what I discovered along my journey. I found a nation with a lot more in common than the network news agencies would admit.

Most folks across the fruited plain really are alike. We work hard, tend backyard gardens, go to high school football games on Friday night, and go to church on Sunday. In a way that's what makes our country so wonderful and the fabric of our freedom so strong.

Consider our countrymen in New Hampshire. They understand the cost of freedom. It's emblazoned on every car in the state: "Live Free or Die." As soon as I crossed the state line from Massachusetts, I found a Cracker Barrel restaurant, picked up a country music station on the radio, and found a NASCAR racetrack. For a minute I thought I made a wrong turn and ended up in Alabama.

In between bites of my all-beef cheeseburger, I contemplated the American narrative—wondering why God chose to shed His grace on this land, on this people. I came up with five reasons.

1. *Country music.* Country music is American music. Johnny Cash, Reba, Dolly, Gretchen, Alabama—the list goes on and on. There's a certain reality to the songs and the singers. I remember after the towers fell on September 11, 2001. There was a lot of frustration and anger in this nation. And it fell to Toby Keith to put all that anger, all that hurt into a song. To this day, "Courtesy of the Red, White, and Blue"[2] is in my iPod. Another thing I appreciate about country music—the women look like women, and the men act like men. I doubt we'll see Charlie Daniels walking around with a man purse.

2. *Guns.* I grew up in the South so I know a thing or two about guns. Unfortunately I live in New York City, where the policies of our elected officials would make one think they'd prefer only the criminals be armed. So these days I have to make do with a can of pepper spray. Thank goodness our forefathers had the wisdom to ensure all Americans have the right to defend themselves, their property, and their nation. And I can only imagine how many countries have thought twice about invading

us, knowing that grandmas across the fruited plain are locked and loaded. In the words of Scarlett O'Hara, "I can shoot straight if I don't have to shoot far."[3]

3. *Barbecue.* A country that knows how to smoke a pork butt is a country worth defending. Friends, our nation is as diverse as the meat it smokes. In the North they smoke hams. In the South we smoke pork. In Texas they smoke beef. In California they smoke pot. Barbecue is not just food; it's a state of mind.

4. *The military.* A few weeks ago New York City celebrated Fleet Week. Hundreds of sailors and Marines were in town to see the sights and reunite with their families. It was a uniquely American moment. Our nation is home to the greatest volunteer military on the planet. How reassuring it is to know young men and women understand our freedom comes with a price. And every day they gladly stand tall so we might stand free.

5. *Freedom.* We are a free people. I'm able to write these words because I am free. We can go to church on Sunday because we are free. We gather in courthouse squares and protest the government because we are free. Sometimes I wonder if we've forgotten about this unique and wonderful gift God has given us. We read the newspapers and magazines and learn America is supposedly in decline—a country that has lost its footing on the international stage. We've seen President Obama stand on foreign soil and apologize on our behalf. Well, quite frankly, who cares what the French or Russians think about us? I'm reminded of the words of Commodore Stephen Decatur. "Our country," he once proclaimed. "In her intercourse with foreign nations, may she always be in the right; but right or wrong, our country."[4]

So there. There we are.

Yet they call us bitter Americans—people who love this country unconditionally, people who pledge allegiance to the flag, people who believe in God, people who go to church, people who volunteer to take up arms and defend our nation against evil, people who believe English should be the nation's official language, people who believe marriage is a covenant before God between a man and a woman. Since when were these such bitter ingredients?

Meanwhile, back inside the Red Arrow Diner, I was polishing off the last bites of my cheeseburger when the waitress suggested I try some dessert.

"Sure. How about some sweet potato pie?"

"Honey, that's a southern dessert. You're in New Hampshire."

"What would you suggest?"

"How about some whoopee?" she asked.

"Excuse me?" I asked, nearly choking on my burger.

The waitress gave me a distressed look and then whacked me on the head with a menu. "It's a pie," she said. "Whoopee pie."

I ordered the pie—with extra whipped cream.

As I sipped on a cup of coffee, I was reminded of the lyrics from that great Lee Greenwood song, "Proud to Be an American":

And I'm proud to be an American, where at least I know I'm free. . . . And I gladly stand up, next to you and defend her still today. 'Cause there ain't no doubt I love this land, God bless the USA.[5]

And that's how I came up with the idea for this book. It's a collection of stories from my travels across this country—conversations I've had with regular folks who have deep concerns about the direction we are going as a nation.

May God bless America, and may He also bless whoopee pie.

Dispatches from DC

1

Laus Deo

 As dawn breaks over the eastern seaboard and the morning sun begins to spill its light across the waters of the Atlantic, there stands a monument of marble and granite rising high above our nation's capital.

The beacon rises more than 555 feet and provides a perfect panoramic of the sixty-nine square miles that comprise the District of Columbia. To the north is the White House; to the south, the Jefferson Memorial; to the west the Lincoln Memorial; and to the east, the Capitol. But no building is as tall as the obelisk.

At its pinnacle is a capstone made of aluminum. It was the intention of her architect, Robert Mills, to carve tributes on all four sides of the capstone; but the message he carved on the eastern side of the monument holds the most importance.

The words have weathered time and turmoil, war and peace. To this day the seven letters Mr. Mills carved into the aluminum capstone remain.

Laus Deo

When morning comes to America, the first rays of light illuminate the capstone and Mr. Mill's testimony for the ages. The obelisk may celebrate a man, but it gives glory to a higher power—Laus Deo—praise be to God.

I thought about the Washington Monument awhile back when I heard the president of the United States deliver a stunning message to the nation and to the world.

President Obama set the record straight on the campaign trail. "America is no longer just a Christian nation," he told the Christian Broadcasting Network.

It would not be the last time he made such a declaration.

"I think that the United States and the West generally, we have to educate ourselves more effectively on Islam," he told a French television station in 2009. "And one of the points I want to make is, that if you actually took the number of Muslim Americans, we'd be one of the largest Muslim countries in the world."

Did you catch that? The president said we'd be one of the largest *Muslim* countries in the world. Wait just a second— I thought the president said the United States was a secular nation?

Obama reiterated his position in Turkey, where 98 percent of the nation is Muslim. The president, standing on foreign soil, declared the United States is not a Christian nation.

"I've said before that one of the great strengths of the United States is, although as I mentioned we have a very large Christian population, we do not consider ourselves a Christian nation, or a Jewish nation or a Muslim nation," he said. "We consider ourselves a nation of citizens who are bound by ideals and a set of values."

The American public, though, disagrees with the president. A Gallup survey found that 78 percent of Americans consider themselves Christian. To be sure, the president has his defenders. Among them is Michael Lind, the editor of *New American Contract*. In a column that appeared in Salon.com, he writes: "President Obama, then, is right. The American republic, as distinct from the American population, is not post-Christian because it was never Christian. In the president's words: 'We consider ourselves a nation of citizens who are bound by ideals and a set of values.' And for that we should thank the gods. All 20 of them."[1]

For what it's worth, John Adams, the second president of the United States, was pretty clear which of the "gods" to thank.

"July 4th ought to be commemorated as the day of deliverance by solemn acts of devotion to God Almighty," he wrote in a letter to his wife, Abigail, on the day the Declaration of Independence was approved by Congress.

Obama's declaration stands in stark contrast to comments once made by former President Ronald Reagan.

"The Founding Fathers believed faith in God was the key to our being a good people and America's becoming a great nation," he said.

And during a National Prayer Breakfast, Reagan did not hesitate to lay out the source of our nation's success. "I also believe this blessed land was set apart in a very special way, a country created by men and women who came here not in search of gold, but in search of God," he said. "They would be free people, living under the law with faith in their Maker and their future. Sometimes it seems we've strayed from that noble beginning, from our conviction that standards of right and wrong do exist and must be lived up to."

Not a Christian nation? Tell that to the men who wrote our Declaration of Independence:

> We hold these truths to be self-evident, that all men are created equal, that they are endowed by their Creator with certain unalienable rights, that among these are life, liberty and the pursuit of happiness.

Not a Christian nation? Tell that to George Washington. He used fifty-four biblical terms to describe God in his various writings. "While we are zealously performing the duties of good citizens and soldiers, we certainly ought not to be inattentive to the higher duties of religion. To the distinguished character of Patriot, it should be our highest glory to add the more distinguished character of Christian," he once wrote.

Not a Christian nation? Tell that to John Jay, the first chief justice of the Supreme Court. "Providence has given to our people the choice of their rulers, and it is the duty, as well as the privilege and interest of our Christian nation to select and prefer Christians for their rulers," he wrote.

Not a Christian nation? Tell that to James Madison, our fourth president and a signer of the U.S. Constitution. "A watchful eye must be kept on ourselves lest, while we are building ideal monuments of renown and bliss here, we neglect to have our names enrolled in the Annals of Heaven," he once wrote.

Not a Christian nation? Tell that to Daniel Webster who once argued before the Supreme Court in favor of teaching religious instruction to children. "What is an oath? [I]t is founded on a degree of consciousness that there is a Power above us that will reward our virtues or punish our vices . . . [O]ur system of oaths in all our courts, by which we hold liberty and property and all our rights, are founded on or rest on Christianity and a religious belief."

Not a Christian nation? Tell that to Patrick Henry, the voice of liberty. "Being a Christian . . . is a character which I prize far above all this world has or can boast," he once said.

Not a Christian nation? Tell that to the father of the American Revolution—Samuel Adams. "I conceive we cannot better express ourselves than by humbly supplicating the Supreme Ruler of the world . . . that the confusions that are and have been among the nations may be overruled by the promoting and speedily bringing in the holy and happy period when the kingdoms of our Lord and Savior Jesus Christ may be everywhere established, and the people willingly bow to the scepter of Him who is the Prince of Peace," he declared in a Fast Day Proclamation in 1797.

Not a Christian nation? Tell that to Benjamin Rush, a signer of the Declaration of Independence and the father of public schools under the Constitution. "The only means of establishing and perpetuating our republican forms of government is the universal education of our youth in the principles of Christianity by means of the Bible," he wrote.

Secular humanists may one day be successful in the religious cleansing of American history. There may come a time when Christian values will be banished from the marketplace of ideas and expelled from our public schools. On the horizon a day fast approaches when Americans could pay a price for following the teachings of Jesus Christ.

And while the winds of change may sweep across the nation's capital, there stands a beacon of hope—a reminder that this nation of immigrants was built not on sinking sand but on a firm foundation, girded by Almighty God. And unless someone has a really tall ladder and a blowtorch, the first rays of morning light will shine down upon these United States of America, illuminating an eternal truth and a grateful nation's prayer. Praise be to God!

Laus Deo.

2

A Conversation
with Mike Huckabee

 Former Arkansas Governor Mike Huckabee is one of my heroes of the faith. We share similar backgrounds.

We are both sons of the South, members of Southern Baptist congregations, and lovers of fried chicken. He also wanted to name Chuck Norris as his secretary of defense. Enough said.

We were recently breaking bread at one of my favorite New York City barbecue joints when the subject of politics and religion came up. Between ribs the governor shared his observations on some topics I believe are important to Christian Americans.

From the VIP booth at Righteous Urban Barbecue, here's a bit of our conversation. And please just ignore the stains; that's just barbecue sauce.

Todd: President Obama once described people who cling to their guns and religion as "bitter Americans." Do you consider yourself a bitter American, and how would you describe people who support gun rights and religion?

Huckabee: Having the capacity to protect myself and enjoy hunting doesn't make me bitter at all—quite the opposite. I'm pretty much a happy guy, and my faith certainly doesn't make me bitter. But then my pastor isn't Jeremiah Wright and hasn't filled me with anger and blame, but grace and forgiveness.

Todd: Some would say it's a defining statement about what President Obama thinks about the rest of the country.

Huckabee: I think it's been clearly evident from his policies that he really does believe in redistribution of wealth. That's frightening because what it shows is a complete lack of understanding of what made America great. He tends to think that our greatness was made by government intervention—to force people to give over what they earn to people who didn't earn it. And that is scary.

Todd: Are you saying there's some sort of disconnect between the White House and the rest of America?

Huckabee: There's no doubt there's a disconnect. But I think it's not just ideological. It's experimental. He has simply not lived as most people have lived. His own childhood and background, his academic life, his adult job experience. He's never run a small business, never met a payroll. He's never signed the front of a paycheck. Those are experiences that would have given him a very different perspective from the one he has.

Todd: Give me your impression of where we are as a country—and where we are headed.

Huckabee: Throughout my lifetime there have been those moments when many thought the country was doomed. It wasn't. When God is ready to close the show, no one can keep it open. When He wants to keep it open, no one can close it.

Todd: Dangerous times?

Huckabee: Dangerous, yes; but hopeless, no. I think this spending that we're engaged in is putting us at a great risk economically for the future. And it's going to result most likely in hyper-inflation, which means the value of things is going to go down dramatically. The impact on the future generations is stark—very, very frightening.

Todd: People are genuinely concerned.

Huckabee: Yeah, they are, and I think rightfully so. Now I'm not a gloom and doomer. I don't think we ought to start burying food in the backyard. I'm not that pessimistic, quite frankly, and the reason being—this is a very resilient country. It also is self-correcting. And for all the talk of how "these are the end of times," how "we'll never live through this again," you know—I've been through this before in my lifetime. The oil embargo, the energy crisis, Vietnam—we've been through so many things, and yet we're still here.

Todd: What is your greatest fear for the nation?

Huckabee: That we would lose hope for our future and act selfishly.

Todd: The statement was made that we are no longer a Christian nation.

Huckabee: We are not a nation that prescribes a faith for us to follow, but to deny that we are based on Judeo-Christian principles is simply to deny history. That's why the Ten Commandments are prominently displayed at the Supreme Court. Read the speeches of George Washington, Abraham Lincoln, and any of the Founding Fathers. You will see the overwhelming evidence of the influence of faith. Of the fifty-six signers of the Declaration of Independence, twenty-seven of them had Bible school or seminary degrees. There were several ministers in that group. So it's absurd when people act as if somehow we are a completely secular nation.

Todd: It seems like many people are disenfranchised with both political parties. What needs to happen in Washington, DC?

Huckabee: We need a total turnover in Congress. We should institute term limits and keep fresh water in the pool.

Todd: There seems to be a lot of hate on both sides of the political aisle. Is it possible for all of us to play nice in the sand-box? Should we?

Huckabee: Of course. It's a matter of enough people without a hidden agenda taking office and acting like adults. That's not likely with the current membership because the wounds are too deep. Pull the handle and flush the toilet!

Todd: So what's a Christian supposed to do?

Huckabee: Christians should stand up for their rights—freedom of speech and freedom of worship. The more we cower in the corner and allow ourselves to be intimidated by the threats of lawsuits, the more freedoms we lose. It's very important that we show up in force and win the fight rather than fail to show up and lose.

3

The Great Barbecue
Bailout of 2010

 WASHINGTON—The president asserted unprecedented government control over the nation's barbecue industry today by authorizing a billion-dollar bailout of pit masters hit hard by an outbreak of swine flu and rising labor costs.

"It's appropriate for the federal government to assume control over the nation's barbecue joints," said Earl Butts, the president's recently appointed Pork Czar. "Who knows more about pork than Congress?"

"Right now our nation's barbecue restaurants are not moving in the right direction fast enough to succeed," said Butts, who warned that the country was on the verge of a pork apocalypse.

"The president has said it before, and I will repeat," he said. "We can't allow pulled pork simply to vanish. We've got to make sure it is there for the pit masters and hog farmers and cardiologists who rely on the industry to stay in business."

Earlier this year the Centers for Disease Control launched a massive campaign to reassure Americans in the wake of the flu outbreak by increasing production of a special swine flu vaccine.

"Americans who took two spoonfuls of barbecue sauce and a side of slaw were able to stave off the symptoms," Butts said.

The Secretary of Health and Human Services held a national press conference to inform the country it was still OK to pull pork. She went so far as to demonstrate how to wipe the sauce from one's mouth—not with your hands but on your shirtsleeve.

However, the damage was already done, leading to the government takeover. It's only the latest in a string of industries to be federalized. Since the early days of the administration, the government has engineered takeovers of Fannie Mae, Freddie Mac, the insurance giant American International Group, and General Motors.

"We cannot afford to see this industry collapse," Butts said. "There is a real concern that could happen."

But some restaurant owners objected to the plan, suggesting pork unions were to blame for the industry's woes.

"Union wages are killing us," said Clyde Marcel, owner of the Memphis-based restaurant, Rib Ticklers. "We're forced to pay our employees on average $75 an hour. We can't pull enough pork to pay the bills."

To cover the cost of wages and pension benefits, many barbecue restaurants have had to pass along enormous price increases to their customers. The average cost of a rack of ribs nationwide is $150, not including wet wipes.

"These pension plans are killing us," Marcel said. "What right do our employees have to live high on the hog? And don't even get me started on the health-care benefits. Do you know how much I'm shelling out for cholesterol coverage?"

As a result, many American consumers have turned to cheaper alternatives, specifically South Korean barbecue.

"It's just not right," said Marcel. "It's bad enough we've got to deal with folks in California who want to barbecue tofu. If the good Lord wanted barbecue to be made in South Korea, he wouldn't have created Memphis."

There is growing opposition on Capitol Hill, as well.

"It crosses a line," said one southern congressman who asked not to be identified. "It's not about saving a way of life. This is about saving the politically powerful pork unions."

Others wonder where the line should be drawn. Should the government save Memphis barbecue or Kansas City barbecue? Wet or dry rub? Carolina mustard or Virginia vinegar?

"This is just a waste of taxpayer money," another lawmaker said. "Pork-barrel spending at its worst, and the president's pork czar is to blame."

Butts was the owner of his own barbecue restaurant prior to his appointment as the White House Pork Czar. He was also the subject of massive protests by animal rights groups after he said the only good animal "is a grilled animal." Regardless, Butts earned the president's affection by perfecting a recipe for barbecuing arugula and was appointed despite congressional opposition.

He deflected criticism of the government bailout and called critics of the program "anti-meat."

"The barbecue industry historically has been the backbone of America's restaurant base," Butts said. "And we're going to do everything in our power to make sure it stays that way."

"The president believes Congress did the right thing, and his attitude is that any additional money we put into the barbecue industry, any help we provide, is designed to ensure a long-term sustainable industry and not just kicking the sauce down the road."

Meanwhile, the White House Poultry Czar is considering plans for an unprecedented bailout of the nation's chicken restaurants. Administration officials have named the project "Cash for Cluckers."

4

The Day They Burned the Bible

 They burned the Bible.

In 2008 American troops confiscated, threw away, and burned God's Word at Bagram Air Base in Afghanistan. The Bibles were written in the Pashto and Dari languages, and the Defense Department was concerned the books might somehow be used to convert Afghans.

The incident became public in 2009. Lt. Col. Mark Wright told CNN such religious outreach could endanger American troops and civilians because Afghanistan is a "devoutly Muslim country."

But there was another reason the Bibles were confiscated. Military rules forbid troops from proselytizing in the country.

"The decision was made that it was a 'force protection' measure to throw them away because, if they did get out, it could be perceived by Afghans that the U.S. government or the U.S. military was trying to convert Muslims," Wright told CNN.

For the back story, read this account from the American Forces Press Service:

> A report broadcast by the Arab news network Al Jazeera about U.S. service members proselytizing in Afghanistan is just plain wrong, Pentagon officials said today.

The Al Jazeera story showed an evangelical religious service on Bagram Airfield in Afghanistan and a discussion about distributing Bibles that had been translated into Dari and Pashto—the two major languages of Afghanistan.

"American service members are allowed to hold religious services," a Defense Department official speaking on background said. "The clip shows one of those services with an American chaplain leading a religious service for American service members. In it, he spoke generically about the evangelical faith. That's all there was to it."

The chaplain did not urge service members to go among the Afghan people and attempt to gain converts to Christianity, the official said.

In the second instance, a young sergeant received a shipment of Bibles translated into Dari and Pashto from his church in the United States. The film showed a discussion about the Bibles. "What it did not show was the chaplain counseling the young sergeant that distributing the Bibles was against U.S. Central Command's General Order No. 1," the official said. The chaplain confiscated the Bibles. "As far as we know, none ever got off base."

Chairman of the Joint Chiefs of Staff Navy Adm. Mike Mullen was asked about the incident—which happened in May 2008—during a Pentagon news conference today. "It certainly is—from the United States military's perspective— not our position to ever push any specific kind of religion, period," Mullen said.

There is no indication disciplinary action was taken against the young service member. "The counseling sufficed," the official said.[1]

So that explains why the Bibles were confiscated and thrown away, but why burn the Holy Scriptures?

Lt. Col. Wright explained to the news network that troops at posts in war zones are required to "burn their trash."

The words I would like to write on this page at this moment are unprintable.

Trash.

Trash.

I can only imagine the anguished Christian soldiers who were forced to toss the Bibles into the roaring fire. I can only imagine what they were thinking as the blaze consumed verses like John 3:16—"For God so loved the world, that he gave his only begotten Son, that whosoever believeth in him should not perish, but have everlasting life" (KJV).

I can only imagine the heartache of the American church that collected the Bibles and sent them overseas to share the good news of Jesus.

So why not just collect the Bibles and send them back to the United States?

The military told CNN they considered doing that. But they worried the church would send them to another organization in Afghanistan, and that would give the impression the Bibles were distributed by the U.S. government.

In other words, the only way to guarantee no Bibles would be found on Afghan soil was to destroy the books.

So how did the Obama administration respond to the revelations of such a horrific act? Allow me to list their responses in chronological order:

There's no need to adjust your reading glasses. The previous two pages are blank for a reason. There was no condemnation from the Bush White House in 2008 or the Obama White House in 2009. There was no condemnation from the State Department. There was no condemnation from the Pentagon.

Perhaps that's to be expected from an administration that believes the United States of America is no longer just a Christian nation.

And that brings us to the story of a tiny church in Florida that decided to burn the Koran.

Reverend Terry Jones generated monster headlines when he announced his intention to burn the Koran. Jones pastors the Dove World Outreach Center, a congregation of about fifty people in Gainesville, Florida.

The nondenominational church planned to host an "International Burn a Koran Day" on the ninth anniversary of the September 11, 2001, terrorist attacks. The protest called Islam a religion "of the devil" and invited others to remember the 9/11 victims and take a stand against Islam.

The reaction from the Obama administration was swift and heavy laden with adjectives.

President Obama called it "contrary to our values as Americans." Attorney General Eric Holder Jr. condemned the plan as "dangerous" and "idiotic." And as *The Washington Times* reported, General David Petraeus warned that burning the Koran would inflame religious tensions and endanger American troops.[2]

The State Department called the church's actions "un-American" and inflammatory. The commanding general of U.S. forces in Iraq, Lloyd Austin III, and Ambassador James Jeffrey called it "disrespectful, divisive, and disgraceful."

Secretary of State Hillary Clinton said, "Acts of disrespect, hate, and intolerance do not represent the American way of life we support and defend and do not reflect the shared values and mutual respect that unite Americans and people of the Middle East. Such provocative acts are an insult to the American tradition of religious tolerance, serve only to fuel and incite violent extremism, and may place the lives of military and civilian personnel serving in the region at greater risk."

And while many Christians would rightly oppose this Koran-burning spectacle on many levels, what stands out is that when I compare the Obama Administration's handling of the dueling book burnings, only one word pops onto my laptop—"hypocritical."

A poll conducted in 2009 by OneNewsNow showed most Americans believed the U.S. government was acting hypocritically by burning the Bible. More than 60 percent believed that "if it had been the Koran, this would never have happened." More than 52 percent of Americans believed the Bible burning was a sign of appeasement toward Muslim countries, and more than 27 percent called it a sign of religious hypocrisy.

"There's really a staggering level of hypocrisy and double standard here for the military to burn the Holy Bible and then complain when a pastor's going to do the same thing to the Koran," said Bryan Fischer, director of issues analysis at the American Family Association. "You know, if the military was going to be fair here and even-handed, they would count up the number of Holy Bibles that they incinerated in Afghanistan, and then they would allow Reverend Jones to burn the same number of Korans."

But something else has been bugging me about this mess. Why is the Obama administration involving itself in the affairs of an American church anyway?

"It is regrettable that a pastor in Gainesville, Florida, with a church of no more than fifty people can make this outrageous and distrustful, disgraceful plan and get the world's attention, but that's the world we live in right now," Clinton was reported as saying in *The Washington Times*. "It is unfortunate; it is not who we are."[3]

What's regrettable is the secretary of state involving herself in the affairs of a Christian church. Mrs. Clinton may not be aware that most Americans would see the burning of the *Bible* as an "insult to the American tradition of religious tolerance."

Most Americans consider flying airplanes into buildings to be an insult to the American tradition of religious tolerance. Most Americans consider massacring American troops at Fort Hood to be an insult to the American tradition of religious tolerance. Most Americans consider trying to blow up a jetliner in Detroit on Christmas Day to be an insult to the American tradition of religious tolerance.

Am I right? Hypocrisy.

"[Certainly] the armed forces should be sensitive to people's religious symbols or their text," Lt. Col. Bob Maginnis (USA-Ret.) told OneNewsNow. "I said at the time [of the Bible burning] that I thought people would go ballistic if the armed forces were to burn Korans.

"Instead of burning the Bibles, there is no reason that they shouldn't have returned them to those who purchased the Bibles," he continues. "But we recognize that in a Muslim country, Christians are just not welcome. The hypocrisy is pretty well established. It is disconcerting."[4]

I was a member of my church's Awana program when I was a little boy. Through Awana I developed a love for the Bible. I memorized dozens of passages of Scripture, tucking away treasured words from God into my heart. That's why I'm so troubled by what happened in Afghanistan.

And that's why I feel compelled to summarize this sad chapter of American history by sharing a passage from the New Testament.

"Jesus wept" (John 11:35).

5

The Pentagon
vs. Franklin Graham

 The son of Billy Graham was banned from the Pentagon's National Day of Prayer over statements he made about Islam after the September 11, 2001, terrorist attacks.

Franklin Graham was invited to speak by military chaplains in 2010. But his invitation was rescinded when Muslim groups complained that Graham called Islam an evil and wicked religion.

"True Islam cannot be practiced in this country," Graham told CNN in 2009. "You can't beat your wife. You cannot murder your children if you think they've committed adultery or something like that, which they do practice in these other countries."

Graham refused to apologize for remarks he made in 2001 and in 2009, leading to outrage among pro-Muslim groups and some Muslim military personnel.

"Speakers such as Franklin Graham reflect a message of religious intolerance, rather than the more American message of differing faiths united in sharing support of our nation's founding principles," Corey Saylor, a spokesman for the Council on American Islamic Relations, told AOL News.

Mikey Weinstein, with the Military Religious Freedom Foundation, told AOL that Graham is an "Islamophobe, an anti-Muslim bigot and an international representative of the scourge of fundamentalist Christian supremacy."[1]

The military quickly rescinded Graham's invitation, noting that his presence at the prayer service might be seen as inappropriate for a government agency.

"We're an all-inclusive military," said spokesman Col. Tom Collins. If that's the case, then why did they exclude Franklin Graham?

Shirley Dobson heads the National Day of Prayer Task Force and defended Graham's participation. "Suggesting Mr. Graham should be removed from a National Day of Prayer event because of his religious opinions is absurd," she said. "No one understands better the need for prayer at this critical juncture in our nation's history.

"Moves to exclude any member of this great family from this prayer event represent everything that is wrong with the agenda of political correctness that is rampant in our country," Dobson said. "Our nation's founders wouldn't have tolerated it, and neither should we."

But Graham hasn't been the only Christian leader targeted by the Pentagon. Tony Perkins of the Family Research Council was scheduled to speak at a national prayer event at Andrews Air Force Base. However, the FRC president was "disinvited" over his opposition to the repeal of "Don't Ask, Don't Tell."

Perkins condemned the decision to ban Graham from the Pentagon prayer event. "Franklin Graham is a man of courage and integrity whose deeply held biblical convictions should not be a pretext for denying him the opportunity to share the gospel," he said. "The fact that he has theological differences with Islam, differences wholly in keeping with the teachings of the New Testament, and that he has expressed them publicly, is now being used by anti-Christian zealots in a manner offensive to the freedom of religion guaranteed by the very Constitution military leaders are sworn to uphold."

Perkins' blistering attack continued: "This decision is further evidence that the leadership of our nation's military has been impaired by the politically correct culture being advanced by this administration. For those Christian leaders who have avoided the controversy of political issues, saying they just wanted to preach the gospel—this should be a wake-up call."

And that's why Georgia Congressman Jack Kingston demanded that Congress investigate the Pentagon's treatment of Christians. "Rescinding the invitations to people as high profile as Franklin Graham and Tony Perkins sends a huge message downstream to all the military chaplains that certain sermons are no longer going to be welcome in the Pentagon circles," Kingston told me. "If you want to get along, you have to go along."

Kingston said Christianity is treated like a "redheaded stepchild" in the nation's capitol and blamed political correctness for the bans on Graham and Perkins.

"If the military says, 'Look, God is no longer welcome; we just want good thoughts by military chaplains,' well that's fine," Kingston said. "But let's have a congressional decision on the matter."

Kingston said military chaplains are also under attack in the Pentagon. The Republican represents a district with four military installations, and he said it's evident there is an aversion to Christianity in official religious services.

"I can tell you the prayers are really no longer prayers," he said. "They are just good thoughts for the day, inspirational messages. But they have very few references to the Lord and you will never hear 'In Christ's name we pray.'"

Former Alaska Governor Sarah Palin gave a vigorous defense of Graham on her Facebook page: "It's truly a sad day when such a fine patriotic man, whose son is serving on his fourth deployment in Afghanistan to protect our freedom of speech and religion, is disinvited from speaking at the Pentagon's National Day of Prayer service."

Congressman Kingston suspects the anti-Christian attitude in Washington is not just limited to the Pentagon.

"The president declared we are no longer a Christian nation," Kingston said. "At best he has a lot of religious ambivalence himself. We're going to have to realize that the Commander in Chief isn't going to stand there for the traditional Judeo-Christian celebrations and observations. At the same time we can't let one person take that away from our history and our traditions in America. The only way that's not going to happen, though, is the people in the pews are going to have to stand up and speak out."

Kingston said Christians should be concerned about recent developments at the Pentagon and that the nation's capitol has almost become a "religion-free zone."

"If Nancy Pelosi and Harry Reid think this is a good thing, let them come out of the closet and say so," he said. "Let's not let this decision be made by Pentagon bureaucrats."

Now, friends, did you ever think you would see the day evangelical preachers would not be welcomed at the Pentagon?

6

Chickens Have Rights, Too

NEW YORK CITY—A federal jury has convicted renowned journalist Todd Starnes of the mass genocide of chickens. Starnes was the first American tried under a new federal law that gives animals the right to sue human beings.

Starnes, who once declared that the only good chicken is a fried chicken, faces twenty-five years in prison. His punishment could have been worse. However, since he only ate white meat, prosecutors were not able to charge him under federal hate-crime statutes.

The jury, made up of a dozen barnyard animals, also found him guilty on aggravated assault charges. According to investigators, several of his victims were battered before being deep fried.

People for the Ethical Treatment of Animals hailed the ruling.

"We proudly stand alongside our poultry brothers and sisters," said a PETA spokesperson. "America's chickens can roost in peace tonight. Their clucks have been heard."

The star witness for the government was Cass Sunstein, the president's livestock czar widely credited with giving animals the right to sue humans—a move that led to the arrest of Starnes.

"Human's willingness to subject animals to unjustified suffering will be seen as a form of unconscionable barbarity," he said, quoting a speech he delivered in 2007 at Harvard University. "It's morally akin to slavery and the mass extermination of human beings."

However, Starnes had several high-profile witnesses in his corner. Among them the Chick-fil-A Cow, who placed his hoof on the Bible and swore to tell the truth.

"Eat more chicken!" the bovine declared, bringing an immediate objection from the prosecution and swift condemnation from Judge Rabinowitz.

"Hate speech against poultry will not be tolerated in this courtroom, not even from a bovine," said the visibly angry judge.

One of the more emotional moments came when Earl the Chicken's widow took the witness stand. She described their life together on the farm and how he taught his chicks that the early bird always gets the worm.

However, defense attorneys raised several questions about her husband's character.

"Isn't it true, ma'am, that your husband was known to associate with other hens in the hen house?"

"Cluck," she clucked.

"And isn't it true that he was known for being something of a hothead—scratching around the barnyard, ruffling feathers?"

"Cluck, cluck," she clucked.

"And furthermore, isn't it true that on the day of his alleged demise, your husband, Earl the Chicken, was a suspect in the mysterious death of a Kentucky colonel known for wearing white suits and black string ties?"

At that point, Mrs. Chicken began squawking uncontrollably. "Ba-gock!"

The judge slammed down his gavel.

"That's it!" he shouted. "I will have order in this court. The chicken is excused—and will the prosecution please instruct your client to refrain from laying eggs in the witness stand?"

After a brief recess to collect the eggs, Judge Rabinowitz

brought back the jury and asked the court reporter to read back some of the bird's testimony.

"I'll do my best, your honor, but it's going to be difficult," she said.

"Why's that, Sally? Forget your reading glasses?"

"No, your honor—it's the writing. It's chicken scratch."

The turning point in the trial came when a forensic scientist from the New York City C.S.I. found what would become the damning evidence against Starnes.

"We searched the defendant's apartment and found what appeared to be the final resting place for Mr. Chicken," said Special Agent Casey Culver. "The evidence was scattered across a kitchen counter—chicken pieces were everywhere. Most had been discarded in a cardboard bucket with red and white stripes."

"Were there any condiments?"

"Not to my knowledge, sir—but we did find a side of slaw."

The prosecutor probed Agent Culver for more information about the crime scene.

"It was one of the most horrendous crime scenes I've ever had to navigate, sir," he said. "We found, we found—I'm sorry—it was just so traumatic."

The prosecutor walked back to his table, grabbed a bottle of water, and handed it to the emotionally distraught agent.

"Take your time, son," he said. "Now, tell us. What did you find?"

"We found appendages sir."

"Appendages?"

"Yes sir. Chicken appendages, and what appeared to be dipping sauces."

The courtroom erupted into a chorus of gasps and several outbursts, leading the judge to gavel the crowd into submission.

"Order!" he said. "I will have order in my courtroom!"

And that's when the special agent dropped the bombshell.

"We found evidence some of the victims were exposed to some sort of chemicals before they were deep fried," said Special Agent Casey Culver.

"What kind of chemicals?" the prosecutor asked.

"We aren't quite certain," Culver replied. "But we've been able to isolate at least eleven herbs and spices."

In spite of the overwhelming physical and circumstantial evidence, Judge Rabinowitz nearly had to declare a mistrial after an unfortunate incident involving the jury. The house cat ate the parakeet, forcing him to install an alternate juror.

It took the jury five minutes to render a verdict.

"Mr. Starnes, you've been found guilty of a most foul crime, the genocide of Earl the Chicken and his offspring. Sir, your behavior is a disgrace to mankind. Do you have any last words before I sentence you?"

Starnes stood alongside his attorney and was immediately surrounded by U.S. marshals. He looked down at the table and then turned to face Judge Rabinowitz.

"Yes, your honor," he replied to a hushed courtroom. "I do have something to say."

"Well, we're waiting," the judge said.

Starnes adjusted his glasses, straightened his tie, and cleared his throat.

"Those chickens were finger-licking good," he replied.

7

Singing Praise Songs to Obama

 "He is the one."[1]

Those were the words uttered by Oprah Winfrey to the people of Iowa. The political savior of whom she spoke was Barack Obama. And on that day he converted many new followers, thanks in part to Oprah's gospel revelation.

In the days following Obama's ascendance to the White House, union educators across the land surrendered to a higher calling—to disciple young boys and girls on the tenets of his political faith, to lead them in the singing of praise songs to the leader they called "the one."

And that brings us to the fine folks at the B. Bernice Young Elementary School in Burlington, New Jersey. Video surfaced showing boys and girls literally singing and chanting President Obama's name.

"Barack Hussein Obama. Mmm, mmm, mmm."

The video showed children repeatedly chanting the president's name and celebrating his accomplishments. At one point the students sang the Christian song, "Jesus Loves the Little Children." But the school's version replaced the name of Jesus with Obama's.

The video set off a firestorm of controversy among parents who claimed the school was indoctrinating their children.

"I'm stunned. I can't believe it's our school," said parent Jim Pronchik. His eight-year-old son was one of the kids on the video. "We don't want to praise this guy like he's a god or an idol or a king or anything like that. That's the wrong message to be sending."

New Jersey's Department of Education ordered a review of the incident, which school officials said was part of a Black History Month celebration.

"I felt this was reminiscent of 1930s Germany and the indoctrination of children to worship their leader," said Robert Bowen in a FOX News interview. He has two children at the school.

But Superintendent Christopher Manno defended the performance telling the *Burlington County Times*, "There was no intention to indoctrinate children. The teacher's intention was to engage the children in an activity to recognize famous and accomplished African Americans."[2]

Now imagine what would happen if a schoolteacher actually wrote a song that was perceived as anti-Obama. What would happen to such a person? For the answer, let me introduce you to Bryan Glover, a now unemployed middle school football coach.

Bryan Glover, an assistant coach at Grassland Middle School near Nashville, cowrote the country music song, "When You're Holding a Hammer, Everything Looks like a Nail."[3] He said the song, which is critical of the president, is the reason he got fired.

It was cowritten by a parent whose child plays on the team. Glover, twenty-six, said he e-mailed a copy of the song to friends, family members, and players' parents through his personal e-mail account.

And that's when all the trouble started for the self-described independent conservative.

"The coach called me and said parents were upset, that I was being politically incorrect and the song had racial overtones,"

Glover told me. "An hour and a half later I was told I was being terminated.

"I was informed that I was being let go because of the song," he said, denying claims there were any racial overtones in the song.

Williamson County School Superintendent Mike Looney disputed Glover's account and said his dismissal had nothing to do with the song.

"Absolutely not," he said. "That's a false claim."

Looney said he was not allowed to go into specifics but acknowledged he spoke with the school's principal and was satisfied with their handling of the matter.

"They presented me with logical, legally defensible reasons for doing so," Looney said. "As far as I'm concerned, they've handled the matter appropriately."

Glover said he's angry over what happened and believes he lost his job because his song was critical of President Obama. And he's not the only one who's angry.

"It was a disgrace, and we have to stand up for the guy," said Michael Katsaitis, who has a son on the football team. He said he met with the principal of the school after Glover's firing and is convinced his dismissal was a result of the song.

"The first thing she told me was that Bryan's song was derogatory to our president," he said. "He shouldn't have been fired over that song."

Glover said he's pretty fired up over his dismissal.

"I'm pretty heated," he said. "I'm just a blue-collar guy, trying to make a living, trying to chase a dream."

So read some of the lyrics for yourself and decide if the school district was justified in their action:

He was a little man, just turned three
Took the present from his daddy's hand
A genuine toy hammer
He started beatin' to beat the band

He hit the floors and the wall, broke a lamp in the hall,
Started swinging at the puppy's tail
When you're holding a hammer
Everything looks like a nail.

He was the president, number 44
He says, "Trust me, I'm here to help you
I have got some big, big plans
You're gonna love what I'm gonna do."
There's no problem too big or small
He thinks he's got an answer that just can't fail
When you're holding a hammer
Everything looks like a nail.

Chorus: He thinks big thoughts and he dreams big dreams
But it's another man's sweat that pays for those schemes
He don't care how the little people feel
'Cause saving the world is a big freaking deal
So he does his business behind closed doors
And pretends that the world is just begging for more
When the stuff hits the fan, he says, "Don't look at me
If you got trouble, blame 43."

There's more, but you get the picture. Political satire. One
man's opinion.

Unfortunately for Bryan Glover, it was one opinion too many.
He got hammered by the nail.

8

The Chocolate Czar

 Brownies are now banned in New York City schools. So are lemon bars, cotton candy—even carrot cake. The Big Apple is cracking down on childhood obesity by outlawing bake sales on school property. It's all part of the education department's efforts to force-feed a wellness policy that also prohibits vendors from selling candy bars and potato chips in vending machines.

According to the mayor's office, about 50 percent of New York City youngsters are overweight. Somebody crunched the numbers and determined that chocolate pudding is making kids stupid, noting the correlation between student health and failing grades on standardized tests.

So now vending machines are stocked with fruit juice and granola bars. And if the cheerleading team wants to earn money for new pom-poms, they'll have to sell carrot sticks and wheatgrass.

School leaders have given principals an incentive to force kids to eat healthy food. "Noncompliance may result in adverse impact on the principal's compliance performance rating," the policy states. In other words, that pudgy kid scarfing Oreos could cost a principal his job.

Howard Wechsler is the director of adolescent and school health at the Centers for Disease Control and Prevention. He told the *New York Post* the city's regulations are among the strictest in the nation. "Schools are supposed to be a place where we establish a model environment, and the last thing kids need is an extra source of pointless calories," he said. For those of you reading between the lines, the good doctor is suggesting that the only place your child can definitely get a well-balanced meal is from the government.

I decided to check in with Smitty, my man down at city hall and the mayor's point person on the candy crisis. Smitty is the director of New York City's Office of Chocolate Control Policy.

He promised to give me an inside look at the underbelly of a burgeoning crisis. So we set up a meeting at Mao Tse Tung Junior High School—ground zero in his quest to eradicate the sugary plague that has befallen our city.

"This is an epidemic," he said. "We believe it goes far beyond the walls of public schools. In many cases children don't get their first taste of chocolate from their friends; they get it from their father or their mother's secret Valentine's Day stash."

"It sounds like a pretty serious problem," I said. "James Bond had Goldfinger, but you've got Butterfinger."

"You don't get it, Todd. America's war on teenage chocolate abuse will be won or lost in our schools. And that's why mandatory testing is necessary. We can't rely on parents to do the right thing, so it's up to the government."

As was the case for drinkers during Prohibition, chocolate lovers have gone underground. And that's certainly the case in the Big Apple. Smitty told me a black market has emerged. Chocolatiers have set up shop in dark alleys and in Central Park, offering kids milk chocolate morsels. The newspapers have been filled with heart-wrenching accounts of youngsters popping Skittles and snorting Pixie Sticks. The problem has become so severe, Smitty has recruited Lindsay Lohan, Britney Spears, and Paris Hilton to produce a series of public service announcements called, "Just say no to Ho Hos."

To illustrate his point, Smitty explained why he wanted to

meet at Mao Tse Tung Junior High School. "We've isolated the heart of the contraband candy industry to this school," he said. "But so far we've been unsuccessful in hunting down the leader."

"Sort of like a Godiva Godfather, I suppose."

"Very cunning," said Smitty. "The product is high grade. Hard to track down. It melts in your mouth, not in your hands."

Many parents and students are upset. They defend the bake sales as a way to raise money for school uniforms and trips. I asked Smitty if extracurricular activities might suffer as a result of the ban.

"Oh, not at all," he replied. "We are providing the schools with some wonderful alternatives to bake sales. For example, children could sell environmentally friendly wrapping paper or adopt a tree."

Adopt a tree instead of nibbling on a Snickerdoodle? Good luck with that.

Our conversation was interrupted by a series of bells and whistles blasting from the public-address system.

"We have a code red in the boy's bathroom. I repeat, code red. Teachers, please lock your classroom doors. All security personnel to your stations!"

Smitty tossed me a Kevlar vest and ordered me to stay close as we sprinted down the hallway.

"What's happening? Has there been a shooting?"

"Worse," said Smitty. "We've got a kid with a candy bar. This might be the break we need."

The bathroom had already been secured by two guards who were busy mounting yellow crime scene tape around the entrance. Smitty flashed his Chocolate Czar credentials and immediately took charge.

"What do we have here, officer?"

"I caught the perpetrator red-handed," he said. "But he wouldn't cooperate so I had to taser the boy."

Sure enough, there was a thirteen-year-old boy convulsing on the floor, his schoolbooks scattered under the urinals.

"Good grief, Smitty. He's just a boy. Was this really necessary?"

"This isn't some sort of schoolyard game, Todd. The War on Chocolate will have casualties. Now somebody cuff the suspect."

Smitty rifled around inside the boy's backpack and pulled out what he thought was the smoking gun, a vial filled with colorful flakes.

"Fruity pebbles?" I asked.

Smitty, disappointed, tossed it aside. "No," he said. "Vitamins. Officer, I thought you said you caught him red-handed?"

"I did, sir. He tried to flush the evidence down the commode."

Smitty flung open the stall door and glanced into the toilet. About thirty seconds later he ordered the officer to release the boy.

"I don't understand, sir. We have the goods on this perp. I caught him before he flushed the candy bar."

"Officer, I'm pretty certain that's not a Baby Ruth floating in there."

There you have it folks. Sometimes you feel like a nut, sometimes you don't.

9

An Inconvenient Truth

 The Great Snow-pocalypse is upon us.

New York City has been attacked by the mother of all snowstorms. AccuWeather dubbed it a "snowicane." For those of you in Des Moines, that's a hurricane with snow. We were told to gird our loins and stock up on bread and Nutter Butters.

The National Weather Service, on the other hand, downplayed the pending doom and preferred to use the term "Winter Storm Warning." They accused their competition of being irresponsible.

"It's almost inciting the public, inciting panic,"[1] meteorologist Craig Evanego told the Associated Press. It's pretty apparent that Craig the weatherman was not in my Brooklyn neighborhood because we had a full-blown snowicane.

It snowed for two straight days, and by the time it was done, New York City resembled a snow globe. More than twenty inches of white stuff, the fourth largest snowfall in Gotham's history. And while most folks hunkered down in their overpriced apartments, news folks, like myself, were called to active duty.

I knew I was in trouble when I had to push open my front door. I knew I was in really big trouble when the door slammed back shut. Trust me, folks. You haven't experienced true Fear Factor unless you've trudged through two feet of snow in a forty-five-mile-per-hour, gale-force wind to make it to the Q-Train subway stop.

The weather was so unbearable even the muggers left me alone. Folks, I had parts of my body shivering I didn't know could shiver. To make matters worse, I think I spotted a wooly mammoth lumbering down the street. Of course, it could've been Snuffleuphagus. I'm not really sure.

It took me about forty-five minutes to walk the four blocks to the subway only to discover the trains were shut down. If I wanted to make it to the office, I was going to have to hoof it—thirteen miles.

So I grabbed an ice pick and some rope and began making my way toward the Coney Island Highway, hoping a stranger might come along on skis to offer me a ride. I was stunned at how the snowicane transformed the landscape of the borough where a tree once grew.

As I traversed the great frozen tundra of Brooklyn, I saw dozens of igloos tagged with fresh graffiti. I watched mothers explaining to their children that the yellow snow was not Italian Ice, and I heard the howls of half-starved native coyotes in search of a meal—although that could've been some of the rap stars who live on Seventh Avenue practicing for an upcoming concert.

Ice, ice, baby . . .

Somewhere near Prospect Park I spotted a group of wayfaring strangers huddled around a trash can that had been set ablaze. As I warmed my hands and nibbled on a frozen Nutter Butter, I paused for a moment to reflect on the calamity that had befallen the Big Apple—this beast of a storm—this snow-pocalypse. I mean, honestly, I thought the scientists told us snowstorms were a thing of the past—near extinction because of global warming.

If you believe the climatologists, we're on a slippery slope to the hothouse. Glaciers are melting, polar bears are homeless, and those cute little dancing penguins are treading water.

"The survival of the United States of America as we know it is at risk,"[2] former Vice President Al Gore told the Associated

Press in 2008. You might remember that the former vice president wrote a book about global warming, *An Inconvenient Truth*.[3] I bought several extra copies just a few days before the snowpocalypse hit. I needed something to weight me down during the blizzard.

Gore wasn't the only one hollering doom and despair. FOX News reported that the head of the National Oceanic and Atmospheric Administration delivered some bad news to the White House.

"The science is pretty clear that the climate challenge before us is very real," said Jane Lubchenco. "We're already seeing impacts of climate change in our own backyards."

That very well may be the case, but how would I know? My backyard was buried under twenty-four inches of snow.

Here's the inconvenient truth: this has been a winter of historic snowfall from coast to coast. They were even building snowmen in Pensacola, Florida—the Redneck Riviera. I hear the locals there are considering putting a bid together to host the next Winter Olympic Games.

As I was contemplating our frigid fate, I managed to catch a glimpse of *The New York Times*, our nation's paper of record. The record snowfall, they opined, was indeed evidence of global warming. It's getting colder, they explained, because the earth is getting warmer. Having trouble following that logic, folks?

I don't want to bore you with all the scientific mumbo jumbo so I decided to conduct an experiment to verify their rationale. I took my nearly frozen copy of *The New York Times*, set it on fire, and whaddya know—global warming!

As bad as it is in New York City, other parts of the nation suffered, too. Places like Atlanta and Akron, Ohio. One poor fellow's house was buried under ten feet of snow. Desperate neighbors reportedly sprayed industrial-sized cans of hair spray directly into the atmosphere hoping to cut through the ozone layer.

Supporters of climate change blame all sorts of calamities on mankind's mistreatment of the earth—from wildfires in

California to the devastating earthquakes that hit Chile, Haiti, and Japan. President Obama told the nation, "We can't control nature."

Well, if that's the case, why are we even debating global warming? Friends, I suspect the inconvenient truth of the matter is that nature was never in control. The Bible is pretty clear that not only did God *create* the heavens and the earth, He also *controls* the heavens and the earth. In other words, throw another log on the fire, make a snow angel, and relax—God is in control.

And here's another inconvenient truth: it's freaking cold out here, y'all.

Snowicane, snow-pocaplyse, call this global warming catastrophe whatever you wish. But if you ask me, it's just a big snow job.

Christmas at the White House

 While most Americans were hauling out the holly, President Obama was about to haul out the baby Jesus. It seems the First Family was planning to celebrate their first Christmas in the White House by having a "nonreligious Christmas."

Former Social Secretary Desiree Rogers reportedly told a gathering of former social secretaries that the Obama family did not intend on putting the nativity scene on display, a longtime East Room tradition.

The account was reported in the Fashion and Style section of *The New York Times*. The White House confirmed to the *Times* that there had been internal discussions about making Christmas more inclusive, but in the end tradition won out, and the nativity scene is once again in its traditional East Room spot.[1]

I called the White House to find out what in the world was going on. They, in turn, directed me to the president's theologically inaccurate speech he delivered at the lighting of the national Christmas tree.

"Tonight, we celebrate a story that is as beautiful as it is simple," the president said. "The story of a child born far from home to parents guided only by faith, but who would ultimately spread a message that has endured for more than 2,000 years—that no matter who we are or where we are from, we are each called to love one another as brother and sister."

In truth Jesus came to save the world. And the message that has endured for more than two thousand years is that "God so loved the world, that he gave his only begotten Son, that whosoever believeth in him should not perish, but have everlasting life" (John 3:16 KJV).

Anyway, all this talk about evicting baby Jesus from the White House has Protestants and Catholics up in arms and, quite frankly, dumbfounded.

"If President Obama wanted to fuel the fears of every serious Christian in American and actually prove that he is every bad thing they've ever heard about him on every crazy Web site, the idea of symbolically taking Jesus out of the White House at Christmas would be just the ticket," wrote Eric Metaxas in a commentary for FOX News.[2]

Bill Donohue, president of the Catholic League, accused the president of trying to "neuter" Christmas. "It should come as no big surprise that he and his wife would like to neuter Christmas in the White House," Donohue said. That's their natural step—to ban the public display of Christian symbols.

"It is the business of the public to hold them accountable for the way they celebrate Christmas in the White House," he added. "We know one thing for sure: no other administration ever entertained internal discussions on whether to display a nativity scene in the White House."

There was a time not so long ago that our elected leaders were unashamed of the glory and majesty of the Christmas season. Consider these words, written by President Reagan and delivered as his Christmas message to the nation in 1981:

Nancy and I are very happy to send our warmest greetings and best wishes to all those who are celebrating Christmas. We join with Americans everywhere in recognizing the sense of renewed hope and comfort this joyous season brings to our nation and the world.

The Nativity story of nearly twenty centuries ago is known by all faiths as a hymn to the brotherhood of man. For Christians, it is the fulfillment of age-old prophecies and the reaffirmation of God's great love for all of us. Through a generous Heavenly Father's gift of His Son, hope and compassion entered a world weary with fear and despair and changed it for all time.

On Christmas, we celebrate the birth of Christ with prayer, feasting, and great merriment. But, most of all, we experience it in our hearts. For, more than just a day, Christmas is a state of mind. It is found throughout the year whenever faith overcomes doubt, hope conquers despair, and love triumphs over hate. It is present when men of any creed bring love and understanding to the hearts of their fellowman.

The feeling is seen in the wondrous faces of children and in the hopeful eyes of the aged. It overflows the hearts of cheerful givers and the souls of the caring. And it is reflected in the brilliant colors, joyful sounds, and beauty of the winter season.

Let us resolve to honor this spirit of Christmas and strive to keep it throughout the year.

Even President Kennedy embraced the true message of the Christmas season. The official White House Christmas card of 1963 was the first to include a religious image. The card featured a color photograph of the nativity scene in the East Room of the White House.

Presidents have actually been sending Christmas cards like these since 1953. But President and Mrs. Obama decided this year's card needed to be more inclusive of the holiday season. So they selected a card that simply said, "Season's Greetings."

The card reads: "May your family have a joyous holiday season and a new year blessed with hope and happiness."

There is no mention of "Christmas," and that has at least one Republican lawmaker a bit puzzled.

"I believe sending a Christmas card without referencing a holiday and its purpose limits the Christmas celebration in favor of a more 'politically correct' holiday," Congressman Henry Brown told me. A few days later he introduced a resolution calling for the protection of the sanctity of Christmas. Dozens of lawmakers, Republican and Democrat, cosigned the bill.

"This kind of reproach is exactly what my Christmas resolution is against," he said. "The resolution expresses support for the use of Christmas symbols and traditions and disapproval of all attempts to ban or limit references to Christmas."

All of this made me decide to call the White House again and follow up on my question regarding the nativity scene issue with a new one about this Christmas card controversy. The hired help said the Obama family celebrates Christmas, but they recognize that other Americans are celebrating other holidays, and they wanted the Christmas card to reflect that idea.

Former President Bush, for his part, was more than glad to acknowledge the reason for the season. In 2008, his final Christmas in the White House, the president and First Lady sent cards including a passage from the New Testament. "Let your light shine before men, so that they may see your good works and give glory to your Father in heaven" (Matt. 5:16).

Barry Lynn is the executive director of Americans United for Separation of Church and State. He said President Obama may be unfairly targeted.

"It makes perfectly good sense for a president of all the people, all the two thousand different religions and the twenty million nonbelievers in this country, to send out a card that says this is a good, happy time of year but without referring to any one specific religion," he said.

I'll keep that in mind the next time the White House sends

me a Fourth of July card that reads, "Season's Greetings." Heaven forbid we offend the British.

But back to the Christmas decorations. I'll admit, it's hard enough decorating my five-hundred-square-foot New York City apartment for the holidays. I can't even begin to imagine how they decorate the White House. Few of us envy the daunting task facing First Lady Michelle Obama—preparing the "People's House" for days of festive parties, tours, and receptions.

So I'm not surprised Mrs. Obama enlisted the services of a decorator to turn the White House into a winter wonderland. I'm only surprised she found her man in Simon Doonan, the creative director of Barneys New York. As described by *The New York Times*, Doonan is "famous for creating naughty yuletide window displays of Margaret Thatcher (as a dowdy dominatrix)."[3]

"Our starting point was a very simple idea," Mrs. Obama said in a White House video, "that we include people in as many places, in as many ways as we can." She wanted to make sure that "everyone feels like they have a place here at the White House."

And by everyone, that includes transvestites and Communist dictators.

The centerpiece of the White House Christmas celebration is the official tree, a Douglas fir rising more than eighteen feet tall. And the 2009 tree was decorated with ornaments depicting Chairman Mao and drag queen Hedda Lettuce.

Just in case you missed the subtlety, folks, the White House Christmas tree was decorated with a murderous dictator and a guy dressed like a woman.

The story was initially reported on Andrew Breitbart's Web site. "This story struck a nerve because it perfectly illustrated an administration that is either tone deaf or has contempt for the millions of Americans who look at Christmas as a traditional Christian holiday," he told the Web site Mediaite.[4]

Well, that about wraps up this Christmastime dispatch from our nation's capital, reporting on what some inside the Beltway are calling Tinselgate. As you sip eggnog and nibble on holiday goodies, I hope your heart finds good cheer in the words of that most wonderful of Christmas songs: "May your days be merry and bright, and may all your Christmases be white."

And by white, I don't mean to be racially insensitive.

11

Baby Jesus, Planned Parenthood, and the White House

 Did the White House really consider removing the nativity from the East Room? It seemed hard to believe. I was still wondering if I'd gotten the full story. But if anyone knew the inside scoop, it was my buddy Smitty. He's a Washington institution. He was in the Beltway before there *was* a Beltway.

Smitty's base of operation is a nondescript coffeehouse a few blocks from the White House. I caught the Delta shuttle from New York City one morning, took a cab from Reagan National Airport, and arrived at the coffee shop to find Smitty sequestered in a corner vinyl booth.

After exchanging pleasantries, I got right to the point: was the nativity scuttlebutt really true?

Smitty's shoulders dropped, and he let out a long sigh.

"That was a difficult situation," he admitted. "There were hours and hours of debate over what to do."

Well, that was a relief. At least it wasn't some sort of rash, last-minute decision.

"Hardly," he said. "The First Lady's social secretary actually commissioned a White House special committee on whether the nativity was politically incorrect. Some of the nation's most well-respected atheists, agnostics, and Wiccans were invited to testify."

I thought it was a bit odd that the committee didn't have any religion experts, but Smitty's explanation seemed to make sense.

"There were some constitutional issues," he said. "We wanted to respect the separation of church and state, but we certainly didn't want to alienate the other side. We reached a compromise by inviting esteemed religion professors from Harvard and Yale to testify."

Initially, he said, the committee had considered keeping some of the main components of the nativity. However, after much debate, that decision was considered problematic.

"Take Mary and Joseph for starters," he said. "We felt like leaving them would send the wrong message to sexually active teenagers."

But didn't Mary give birth to her child? Doesn't the Christmas story contain a pro-life message?

"Exactly," he said, pausing to take a sip of coffee. "And that was Planned Parenthood's point. So we decided it would be appropriate to remove Mary and Joseph."

What about the three wise men?

"Affirmative action issues," he replied. "There were also some concerns about diversity. Why were the only wise people *men*? Could there not have been a wise Latina? And don't even get me started on what happened with the shepherds."

I couldn't imagine what issues the White House would have had with shepherds tending their flocks.

"They weren't union," Smitty replied.

Based on my recollection of the Gospel of Luke, that left only a handful of characters, most notably the angels.

"Yeah, a chorus of flighty guys wearing dresses," Smitty said as he removed his glasses. "I don't need to tell you about the issues involving those stereotypes."

It seemed as though the only politically correct part of the nativity was the livestock.

"Well, that's what we thought, too," he replied, as he wiped his glasses with a handkerchief. "The People for the Ethical Treatment of Animals signed off on the plan. They said it appeared the animals were well cared for. But then we received a cease and desist order from the Environmental Protection Agency."

The EPA?

Smitty motioned for me to move closer. He looked to his left, then his right before whispering in my ear. "It had something to do with the sheep," he said.

The sheep?

"According to a new government study, sheep pose a significant danger to the environment," he replied. "Our scientists have determined a twenty-pound sheep can release the equivalent of thirty-seven pounds of carbon dioxide."

Sheep gas? The federal government actually commissioned a study on sheep gas?

"It's nothing to joke about," he said. "A twenty-pound gassy sheep could blow a hole in the ozone."

By the end of the day, the White House special committee on whether the nativity was politically incorrect eliminated Mary, Joseph, the wise men, the shepherds, the angelic choir, and the sheep. The only remaining component of the nativity was the most important, and according to Smitty, it was the first to go—the baby Jesus.

"That was a no-brainer," Smitty said. "Religion has absolutely no place in the nativity."

And one would assume that was the end of the story, but we know that something miraculous happened in that meeting, something that saved the Christ child from eviction.

"You can thank Fannie Mae and Freddie Mac," he said. "Can you imagine the political ramifications of evicting an impoverished young family in this economy? The powers that be thought it would send an insensitive message to the electorate to do something like that, especially during the holiday season."

So that's the news from the nation's capital, friends—at least the way it was told to me. The nativity is safe for at least another yuletide season. But next December, don't be surprised if the folks at 1600 Pennsylvania Avenue are singing "Away with the Manger."

12

Prayers from a Gutter

The boys and girls traveled more than twenty-three hundred miles. They came to Washington, DC, to see their nation's capitol—to walk among the statues honoring the greatest of our patriots, to gaze upon the monuments to freedom's greatest moments.

And the students from an American history class at Wickenburg Christian Academy in Arizona also came to pray. The young Christians were demonstrating the lessons they learned—to pray for the nation, to pray for her leaders, and to petition the Almighty for His continued blessings.

The small group had just taken a photograph on the steps of the Supreme Court building when the teacher, Maureen Rigo, gathered them to a side location. They formed a circle and on May 5, the day before the National Day of Prayer, they began to pray.

"It was just supposed to be a time that we could pray quietly for the Supreme Court, for the decisions they need to make and for our congressmen," she said. "We kind of feel like our government can use all the prayers it can get."[1]

Within a matter of moments, an armed police officer "abruptly" interrupted the prayer and ordered the group to cease and desist.

Nate Kellum, senior counsel with the Alliance Defense Fund, told me it was an incredulous moment. "They were told to stop praying because they were violating the law and they had to take their prayer elsewhere," he said.

Mrs. Rigo, the American history teacher, was stunned, and several of her students were overcome with emotion.

"I was pretty shocked because we've prayed there before and it's never been an issue," she said. "His (the police officer's) comment was, 'I'm not going to tell you that you can't pray. You just can't pray here.'"

So the group of fifteen students and seven adults obeyed the police officer and did as they were instructed. They left the Supreme Court and relocated to a sidewalk where Mrs. Rigo said the children stood in a gutter and continued their prayer.

"It's an outrage of the first magnitude," said Congressman Trent Franks, a Republican from Arizona. The school is in his congressional district.

"When the day comes that people at the Supreme Court press children off into the gutter before they can pray, it portends a very frightening future for this country," he told me.

"This police officer acted reprehensibly," Franks said. "Those students had every right to pray there on the steps of the Supreme Court."

The Alliance Defense Fund sent a letter to the Supreme Court urging them to stop their police officers from banning prayers. And a spokesperson for the Court said the marshal of the court will look into the events alleged by the ADF.

"The Court does not have a policy prohibiting prayer," said public information officer Kathy Arberg in an e-mail.

"The Court's policy regarding the use of most public areas at the Court has been to permit activity related to the business of the Court, including traditional tourist activity and ingress and egress for visitors but not to permit demonstrations and other types of activity that may tend to draw a crowd or onlookers," she said. "In addition, under 40 U.S.C. section 6135, it is unlawful to

parade, stand, or move in processions or assemblages in the building and grounds, including the plaza and steps, but not including
the perimeter sidewalks."

But Kellum said the fifteen students and seven adults did not
constitute a parade.

"From what we gather, the police officer at the Supreme
Court building determined that because they were bowing their
heads, they were bringing notice to their Christianity, which they
considered a movement and thus violating this federal statute,"
he said.

Congressman Franks said he worried about the message it sent
to the young children.

"I hope somehow this injustice is brought right," he said.
"These kids shouldn't grow up thinking that it's all right to stand
by and let that happen to them. Their courage may keep it from
happening not only to other children but may be some sort of
example to the nation."

Bob Ritter, staff attorney for the American Humanist
Association and a member of the Supreme Court Bar, said he
doesn't believe the police officer's action had anything to do with
an attack on religion.

"The policy would be that a group of people would not be
able to amass on the steps for security reasons," he said. "But this
would not have anything to do with praying."

Rigo said she decided to use the events of last May as a learning experience for her young students.

"We do a long study on the U.S. Constitution," she said. "We
talked about the rights given to us in the First Amendment—the
right to freedom of speech, the right to freedom of religion. We have
the right to peaceful assembly. We have the right to due process of
law. We feel like all of those things had been denied us there."

And so it was on a warm spring day that a group of boys and
girls from Arizona gathered together in a gutter to petition God
to bless this nation on the eve of the National Day of Prayer.

May God have mercy on us indeed.

13

Walk toward the Light

I've been feeling a bit under the weather lately so I decided to drop by my doctor's office for a quick checkup. I've been going to the same physician for quite some time so you can imagine my surprise when I discovered his office was shuttered. There was a "For Sale" sign on the window and tumbleweeds blowing across the parking lot.

On the front door was a note:

To my faithful patients,

Thank you for many years of support. Sadly, I have decided to close my practice. After the government takeover of the health-care industry, it became clear that I would no longer be able to support my family as a private physician. I encourage you to visit the community's official government-sanctioned health-care facility around the corner. Just look for the sign with the giant yellow M.

I hope you will visit me at my new place of employment. I'm a barista at Starchucks Coffee House.

Sincerely,

Doc

What a shocker! I knew some doctors were having a hard time making ends meet, but geez! I walked around the corner, and sure enough, there was a gleaming red and chrome building. Out front was the giant yellow sign: McQuack. "Over 200 million served and dropping."

I walked inside and was warmly greeted by a pimply faced teenager with braces.

"Hi, I'm Trudy. Welcome to McQuack. How may I serve you today?"

"I'd like to see a doctor, please."

"Just place your finger in the biometric scanner, and McQuack will be glad to take care of you," she said.

I did as I was instructed when suddenly the scanner began buzzing and blinking red.

"Sir, I'm afraid your genome has been declined."

"What does that mean?" I asked.

"It means you don't have an appointment to see a McQuack physician."

"Can I make an appointment?"

"It's not that simple," she said. "The next opening we have is in about eighteen months."

"Eighteen months? But I have the sniffles now. What am I supposed to do?"

"Well, if you needed lip augmentation or a back wax, we could fit you in right away."

"My lips are fine," I protested, "it's my allergies, and I really need to see someone."

"Then I should probably direct you to the McQuack super value menu where you can be seen by a member of the American Corps of Registered Nurses, also known as ACORN."

"Uh, what else do you have?"

"We can hook you up with a health associate from the Civilian National Security Force."

I decided to take my chances with the health associate. I was led into a small, windowless room where I was given a government-issue hospital gown and told to strip to my skivvies. A few minutes later a fresh-faced fellow walked into the room holding an iPad.

"Good afternoon, sir. I'm Johnny, your friendly neighborhood Internal Revenue Service professional health-care associate. How may I be of service?"

Wait a second, I thought to myself. *I know this guy.*

"Johnny?"

"That's my name, sir."

"Johnny the pizza guy?"

"Mr. Starnes? Is that you?"

"What the heck—you delivered a pizza to me last week."

"Ain't life crazy? Last week I delivered a vegetarian pizza to a community organizer in Brooklyn and got offered this job as a friendly neighborhood Internal Revenue Service professional health-care associate. Isn't this an amazing country? So what seems to be your trouble?"

He listened intently as I described my sniffles, taking notes on his iPad while shaking his head.

"Now according to your last Internal Revenue Service audit, you've been treated for high blood pressure, irritable bowel syndrome, and acid indigestion."

"That's correct," I replied. "It sort of hit me after the last general election, but I'm feeling much better."

"That's good to hear, Mr. Starnes, but I'm afraid we may have a problem. The Internal Revenue Service only allows three health credit deductions per American," he said. "According to our records, you've reached the limit."

"And that's a problem?"

"I'm afraid it is, sir. Under the government's new three-strikes-you're-out law, you've already reached your health credit limit."

"For this month?"

"No, sir. For your life."

"I don't think I'm following you."

"It means McQuack can't treat your sniffles," he said.

I was stunned. "What do you mean you can't treat me? I thought we were supposed to have access to the best health care on the planet! I read the bill—all 248,000 pages. I thought government-funded health care was a God-given right. I thought it was supposed to provide me universal health care, build jungle gyms, cure urban blight in Scranton, Pennsylvania, and provide Viagra to sex offenders?"

Johnny the pizza guy let out a deep sigh and said, condescendingly, "And do we believe in the tooth fairy, too, Mr. Starnes?"

"There must be a mistake," I stammered.

"Mr. Starnes, I am a highly trained health-care associate employed by the Internal Revenue Service. I can assure you McQuack does not make mistakes."

"Look, all I have is a case of the sniffles," I said. "Just give me some allergy medicine, and I'll be on my way."

"It's not that simple, Mr. Starnes. This was a complicated algorithm. First, we examined your computerized medical records. Then we consulted with the government's mandated health-care guidelines. We took that information and factored in your life expectancy, multiplied that number with your carbon footprint, and finally we divided that number by your earning potential."

"So what are you telling me?"

"You probably shouldn't have had that large pepperoni pizza with extra cheese last week."

It took a few minutes to understand what was happening.

"Sweet mercy! You're sending me to a death panel, aren't you?"

Johnny the pizza guy smiled and shook his head. "Oh, that's just a bunch of right-wing propaganda," he said. "There are no death panels, no grim reapers. Here at McQuack, it's just plain old BOB."

"Who's Bob?"

"BOB is a what," he said. "It stands for Board of Bereavement, and as we've been chatting, BOB has been plotting your future."

"And what's the verdict?"

"Well, Mr. Starnes, you love your country, don't you?"

"Of course I do."

"Well, BOB believes the most patriotic thing you can do is stop breathing."

"But I've only got the sniffles, and you're telling me I'm doomed?"

"It's for the good of the country, Mr. Starnes," said Johnny the pizza guy.

I started getting a bit misty. So this was it. I was about to meet my Maker. "Could I at least visit with a minister?"

"Umm, that's going to be a problem—separation of church and state being what it is. I'm sure you understand."

Johnny the pizza guy patted me on the back and thanked me for the generous tip I had given him the previous week.

"I can see you are a bit apprehensive, but you don't have to worry about a thing. We've made amazing advances in pharmaceuticals that help transition health consumers like yourself into the great abyss. At no additional cost to your survivors, the government is willing to provide you with cessation treatments in either pill or liquid form."

"So what are you telling me?"

"You can either drink the Kool-Aid or bend over," he replied.

Does the President Have a Jesus Problem?

 The nonpartisan Pew Research Center released a survey that indicates a growing number of Americans have doubts about the president's religious beliefs. And while it's not my business to say one way or the other, the issue is worth exploring merely for the fact that a leader's conduct and decision-making will always be influenced by what he or she believes at the core. A nation deserves to know what they can expect.

Faith and practice may be able to stay isolated from one another in theory, but they are joined too closely at the heart to walk in totally separate paths.

Here in a nutshell is the mood of the people: The Pew poll shows nearly 18 percent of Americans believe Obama is Muslim. That's up from 11 percent the previous year. A survey by *TIME* magazine positions the number even higher at 24 percent.[1]

Only 34 percent, on the other hand, believe Obama is Christian, down from 48 percent the year before. In other words, as much as 66 percent of the country believes the president is either not a Christian or doesn't know. And the numbers are growing.[2]

The president, however, refutes the feeling of the American majority. Addressing matters of faith during a prayer breakfast in the nation's capital, he said, "My Christian faith . . . has been a sustaining force for me over these last few years—all the more so when Michelle and I hear our faith questioned from time to time. We are reminded that ultimately what matters is not what other people say about us but whether we're being true to our conscience and true to our God."

OK. I can live with that. I've always been one to take a man at his word. "Do not judge, so that you won't be judged" is how the Scripture reads (Matt. 7:1).

All I'm asking is what I believe to be a fair question: Why the confusion? What accounts for the distance between what the president says and what much of the country perceives? A reporter ought to be able to look curiously and objectively into a plausible answer for that.

A series of incidents may give evidence for the uncertainty.

For starters, does anyone remember the Reverend Jeremiah Wright? The good reverend was President Obama's pastor for twenty years. He married the president and his wife, baptized their daughters, and was given credit for the title of Obama's book, *The Audacity of Hope*.[3]

But the Reverend Wright's comments after the September 11, 2001, terrorist attacks seem to be etched in people's memories. He delivered a fiery sermon from the pulpit of Chicago's Trinity United Church of Christ suggesting the United States had brought on al Qaeda's attacks because of its own terrorism. "America's chickens are coming home to roost," he thundered.

For those of us who live in the fly-over states, such comments and sentiments are simply hard to fathom. Most of us immediately after 9/11 were in churches where prayers were offered for those who died and those who were injured. We prayed for our nation and our leaders. We sang worship songs and asked God to protect our people. We collected offerings and donations and sent missionary teams to help clean up and repair the damage of that terrible day.

And yet in President Obama's church, there was simply

condemnation—of our own country. Loud, profanity-laced ser-
monizing with the anger pointed at us instead of our cold-blooded
enemies. If the pastor of the local First Baptist Church had
uttered such vile language, I suspect the chairman of deacons
would have led an armed delegation to the pulpit and ordered him
to vacate the building.

Granted, President Obama told *The New York Times* he was not
in attendance during the terrible comments made after 9/11. And
once audio of the sermons became a campaign issue, he left the
church and denounced his former pastor's remarks. Yet the truth
remains he sat under such teaching for twenty years. And one can
only wonder how this may have affected his personal views and
positions.[4]

Still, there have been other issues and actions to stir doubts.

• During an interview with *The New York Times*, Obama
recited the opening lines of the Arabic call to prayer with what
columnist Nicholas Kristof described as a "first-rate accent,"[5] noting this revelation might not set well with people in Alabama.
"Mr. Obama described the call to prayer as 'one of the prettiest
sounds on Earth at sunset,'" Kristof wrote. For many Americans
the prettiest sound on Earth might be Sunday school children
singing "Jesus Loves Me."

• The White House omitted the traditional phrase "in the
year of our Lord" on a presidential proclamation declaring May
as Jewish American Heritage Month. Instead, the final paragraph
read, "the thirtieth day of April, in the year two thousand ten."
This decision marks a significant change in White House tradition. Both President Clinton and President Bush signed similar
declarations with the traditional "in the year of our Lord" closing.

• President Obama dropped the words "by their Creator"
when reciting a key excerpt from the Declaration of Independence to the Congressional Hispanic Caucus.[6] "We hold these
truths to be self-evident," he quoted, "that all men are created
equal, endowed with certain unalienable rights: life, liberty and
the pursuit of happiness." The actual quotation, of course, states

that they are "endowed *by their Creator* with certain unalienable rights." Easily explained coincidence? Unfortunate oversight? Yet a few weeks earlier, during a speech delivered at a fund-raiser for the Democratic Congressional Campaign Committee, the president had already begun this habit of omitting the word *Creator* when referring to this passage.

• The Obama administration is opposing the commemoration of a prayer by Franklin D. Roosevelt at the site of the World War II Memorial on the Washington Mall. The prayer, entitled "Let Our Hearts Be Stout," was delivered and broadcast to the American people on the evening of June 6, 1944, at the very moment U.S. troops were storming the beaches of Normandy. Officials from the Bureau of Land Management say the inscription of this prayer would "dilute this elegant memorial's central message" and would violate a policy designed to avoid adding new elements to existing monuments—an act that has been overridden at other times, for example, by adding an inscription of the "I Have a Dream" speech at the Lincoln Memorial. Ohio Rep. Bill Johnson, sponsor of the project to be funded by private donations, cannot believe he is meeting with rejection from the White House. "For there to be objections to demonstrating a faith in God at critical points in our nation's history—particularly D-Day—boggles my mind," he said.[7]

Here's another. In preparation for a scheduled presidential speech at Georgetown University in 2009, the White House asked the school to cover up all religious signs and symbols prior to the event. "The White House wanted a simple backdrop of flags and pipes and drape for the speech,"[8] University Spokesperson Julie Green Bataille told CNS News.

Georgetown is a Jesuit college, one of the most prestigious Catholic institutions of higher learning in the country, and therefore boasts a wide number of religious artifacts and etchings scattered across the campus. Inside Gaston Hall, for example, where President Obama was supposed to speak, the monogram "IHS" adorned the stage.

Interestingly, former First Lady Laura Bush spoke in the same hall at Georgetown in 2006. The Bush Administration made no requests for the religious symbols to be hidden.

Yet the university complied with the White House demands to secularize the Catholic campus—a decision that came under fire from Catholics who accused officials of selling out its Catholic identity. "The cowardice of Georgetown was appalling last year, and the continued spin tells us all we need to know about what is going on there," said Bill Donohue of the Catholic League.

The incident did nothing, however, to assuage people's doubts about the president.

Taken together with such reports as mentioned earlier about his administration's desire to remove the baby Jesus from the East Room of the White House at Christmastime, it's just a lot to wrestle with.

Like I said, it's confusing to people.

I decided if I was going to get to the bottom of this matter, I needed to call my man Smitty. He's the insider of Washington insiders. And I knew he would shoot straight with me about the "Jesus issue" at the White House.

I received a rather cryptic message from Smitty telling me to meet him at St. Largess Catholic Church, a popular worship place among Democratic and Republican lawmakers alike.

When I arrived, he ushered me into a confessional booth, closed the curtains, and began to spill the beans about what was being done behind the scenes to counteract the problem.

"It really is a source of frustration," Smitty said. "The president is obviously a Christian. He prays every day."

I told Smitty he might want to check his theology on that.

"But we understand it's going to take more for the American people to embrace the president's unique approach to faith so we've started thinking out of the box," he said.

"How far out of the box?"

"Well," Smitty said, "I'm really not sure if I should share this information with you. It's top secret. Not even Jay Carney has it."

"Oh, come on, Smitty. You can trust me. I'm a reporter."

Smitty motioned for me to scoot closer to the confessional box screen.

"We've launched a special government task force—code name: Operation Jesus Freak," he said. "Our special ops team is made up of the nation's best Christian marketing firms, self-help gurus, and television evangelists."

Operation Jesus Freak?

"From the dc Talk song, 'What would people do if they knew I was a Jesus Freak,'" Smitty said. "The president is much more engaged in matters of faith than the average American. That's why he rarely refers to Jesus or God by name."

So how is Operation Jesus Freak supposed to help the commander in chief?

"We've worked up a full game plan. It's going to be an all-out assault on Christian America," Smitty said. "By the time we get finished with this marketing plan, the nation will think of the president as the next Billy Graham."

"He's going to do crusades?"

"Minus the crusades. This president doesn't do crusades."

So what can the average American expect from Operation Jesus Freak?

"Well, some of the components are already in place," Smitty said. "His new book, *The Purpose Driven Presidency*, will be released in a few weeks.

"And we've also plastered the presidential limousine with a 'Honk If You Love Jesus' bumper sticker," Smitty said. "By the way, did you catch the presidential seal inside the White House Press Briefing Room?"

"I must have missed it," I replied.

"If you look closely—just underneath the White House—you'll see the Jesus fish," Smitty said.

"Do you really think a bumper sticker and a subliminal Jesus fish are going to sway public opinion?"

"No, that's just the first wave of Operation Jesus Freak,"

Smitty said. "The big stuff happens at the end of his next State of the Union address."

"What's going to happen?"

"The president is going to hold an altar call," Smitty said. "It's brilliant!"

Smitty also rattled off some other details. The entire First Family will begin wearing WWJD bracelets, and White House Press Secretary Jay Carney will start recognizing reporters by giving them a faith-healer slap across the forehead.

There's also talk of replacing the Marine Corps Band with a worship team. Smitty also mentioned the possibility of the president's covering "Let the Eagle Soar," a song written by former Attorney General John Ashcroft.

"The president has a lovely singing voice," Smitty said.

We may also see a more laid-back president. Smitty told me the church-marketing experts suggested our commander in chief shed his suit coat and tie.

"Focus groups tend to enjoy leaders who dress down," Smitty said. "We're suggesting Hawaiian shirts, khaki pants, and sandals."

Even the White House is undergoing a makeover.

"It's just too formal, too traditional," Smitty explained.

"But it's the White House," I countered. "It's *supposed* to be traditional."

"Not any more, Todd. We've decided to rebrand the White House."

"What?"

"Starting in two Sundays, it will be called 'The House on Pennsylvania Avenue,'" he said.

But Smitty said Operation Jesus Freak could all depend on one single issue—the president's passion for Sunday morning golf.

"He's got to stop it, Todd," he said. "I mean what kind of a churchgoing American Christian would play golf on a Sunday morning? What would people think?"

Well, come to think of it, I suspect people would think that the president is behaving just like an average American Christian.

Dispatches from the Fly-over States

15

The War on Christmas

 For those of you who thought the war on Christmas was over, or that its battle lines were contained to Washington, DC, celebrations, let me offer this observation.

You're wrong.

Santa Claus has been banished, Christmas carols like "Away in a Manger" and "Silent Night" have been outlawed, and baby Jesus has been kicked to the curb as anti-Christian forces conduct a religious cleansing of our public schools and courthouses all over the land.

The school board in the town of Tewksbury, Massachusetts, voted unanimously to banish "Christmas" vacation over the objections of citizens.

"Who got offended now?" Mary Firth wondered. "It concerns me that you start with this, and who knows where it stops."

Boys and girls at Connecticut's Walsh Elementary School are forbidden from uttering the words "Merry Christmas." A grade school in East Syracuse, New York, has evicted Jolly Old Saint Nick from the lunchroom. The school district says while Santa may be a secular icon, he's too closely connected to Christmas.

And holiday censorship is not limited to the Northeast or Pacific Northwest. Consider the state of Texas—where every other person is a Baptist.

The Texas Education Agency actually considered dropping Christmas from lesson plans that would teach sixth-graders about the world's major religions. They were going to drop Christmas, people! In its place the intellectual elitists wanted to put in Dwali—don't ask.

Is it political correctness on crack, or is something more sinister at work? I'll let you decide after reading these dispatches from the front line of the battle to save Christmas.

Santa Is a Nazi

If you thought the Grinch stole Christmas, then you haven't been to Byam Elementary School in Chelmsford, Massachusetts. They bring new meaning to the term "War on Christmas."

Every yuletide season, the school's PTO organizes a holiday shop. But they may as well be selling toilet paper because the volunteers aren't allowed to sell anything that might remind shoppers of Christmas.

The gift shop banned Santa, candy canes, stockings, and any other "religious items." Even red and green tissue paper are no-no's, said Kathryn McMillan. She has a child who attends the school. The tissue paper was forbidden, she said, because it looked too "Christmassy."

Needless to say, Kathryn was livid so she teamed up with another parent and made her concerns public. It only made things worse.

"One of the parents said, 'If we allow Santa, what do we say if a child brings a swastika? Do we allow that, too?'"[1] she told the *Lowell Sun* newspaper.

The answer, of course, is to give the kid a swift kick in the behind and tell him about baby Jesus, but then again I'm not a professional educator so what do I know?

"All I could think of was, are you kidding?" she said. "You're comparing a Christmas ornament to a swastika? It seems as if reason is lost somewhere, and I just hope we can find it again."

Good luck with that.

Bill Donohue, president of the Catholic League, is among those sickened by the mess. "Some may see this as simply absurd," he said. "We don't. We see it as pernicious: in the name of diversity and inclusion, the multicultural tyrants get to do what they have always wanted to do—censor Christmas."

In the meantime the anti-Christmas Gestapo rules the day in Chelmsford, Massachusetts.

Jesus or the Snowman?

Bellview Elementary School in Ashland, Oregon, is all about feelings. That's why Principal Michelle Zundel decided to ban the school's annual Christmas "giving tree."

"The Christmas tree, while a secular symbol, according to the Supreme Court, does symbolize Christmas," she told KTVL-TV. "And if you are entering a public school and your family does not celebrate Christmas, then it feels like a religious symbol."[2]

And of course we all know the story of Joseph and Mary exchanging presents under the Christmas tree at the Bethlehem Motel 6.

You might be wondering what was so nefarious about the Bellview Elementary School Christmas tree. It turns out the tree was adorned with snowmen—tagged with the name of a gift that would be given to a needy child.

Allison Hamik is responsible for the giving tree. She's pretty fired up over all this mess. "I don't see it as a religious symbol," she said. "I see it as part of our cultural traditions of the holiday season."

In the end Principal Zundel uprooted the Christmas tree and tossed it to the curb—along with Santa Claus. (I suspect they believe he was at the birth of Jesus, too.) In their place she erected two giant snowmen, and brace yourself for the reason: "A snowman is created by children at play in the snow," the principal told the local television station. "So it doesn't have a particular religious bent."

I always thought Frosty was an Episcopalian, one of the frozen chosen.

Children Singing Praises to Allah

A battle over religion is brewing in central Indiana after a public school wanted second-graders to sing a song declaring, "Allah is God." The phrase was removed just before the performance after a national conservative group launched a protest.

The principal of Lantern Road Elementary School in Fishers, Indiana, said they were trying to teach inclusiveness through their holiday production. It included references to Christmas, Hanukkah, Ramadan, Las Posadas, and Kwanzaa. However, no other deity, other than Allah, was referenced in the show.

"It went off . . . without a hitch," Danielle Thompson told *The Indianapolis Star*. "Several families thought it was a nice program."[3]

But others did not, especially David Hogan. His daughter came home with a copy of the lyrics just days before the production. Hogan, a Christian, told the American Family Association, a conservative advocacy group, that he was deeply concerned to learn his daughter had been singing, "Allah is God."

Here's what the children were assigned to sing:

Allah is God, we recall at dawn,
  Praying 'til night during Ramadan
  At this joyful time we pray happiness for you,
  Allah be with you all your life through.

But when it came time to perform the "Christian" part of Christmas, children were assigned to say:

I didn't know there was a little boy at the manger. What child is this?
  I'm not sure if there was a little boy or not.
  Then why did you paint one on your nativity window?
  I just thought if there was a little boy, I'd like to know exactly what he (sic) say.

Micah Clark, executive director of the Indiana AFA, launched an Internet protest once he heard about the allegations. "What surprised me here is that we've had a secular scrubbing of Christmas for so long and the school apparently didn't see the problem with kids singing to Allah," he told FOX News Radio. "You won't even mention Jesus, and you're going to force my child to sing about Allah?"[4]

In e-mail correspondence the school initially defended the reference as a way to be inclusive of all religions. However, once complaints starting rolling in, school leaders decided to eliminate the Allah reference.

This drew the ire of the Muslim Alliance of Indiana. "It's unfortunate if that was removed from the program just because of Islamophobic feelings," Shariq Siddiqui told *The Indianapolis Star*. "Schools are a place where we should learn more about each other rather than exclude each other based on stereotypes and misconceptions."[5]

But Clark said having children bow and pray is problematic for non-Muslim families. "[This show] affirmed Islam and negated Christianity. I wouldn't have had a problem if it had been equal to all faiths."

Judge Affirms Ban on Christmas Carols

"We Three Kings of Orient" are no more, thanks to three judges in Philadelphia.

The Third Circuit Court of Appeals has upheld a New Jersey school district's ban on Christmas carols, despite admitting in its ruling, "Certainly, those of us who were educated in the public schools remember holiday celebrations replete with Christmas carols and possibly even Hanukkah songs, to which no objection had been raised."

The controversy surrounds a 2004 decision by the Maplewood-South Orange School District to ban religiously themed carols. It also banned the high school gospel choir from performing at a school assembly.

The ban went so far as to forbid a school brass ensemble from performing instrumental versions of religious holiday songs. The lawsuit against the school was filed by a parent who argued his children's First Amendment rights had been violated.

But the appeals court sided with the school district, writing: "Since then, the governing principles have been examined and defined with more particularity. Many decisions about how to best create an inclusive environment in public schools, such as those at issue here, are left to the sound discretion of the school authorities."

In other words, folks, the times they are a-changing.

Run, Rudolph, Run

Rudolph the Red-Nosed Reindeer is too religious. That's the allegation from the mother of a child who attends Murrayville Elementary School in North Carolina. She was especially upset because the song included the words *Christmas* and *Santa*. The song had been included in the annual "holiday" concert performed by kindergartners.

The miffed mom told the *Wilmington Star News* she wanted to have a Hanukkah song added to the musical lineup.[6] However, Hanukkah Harry did not make the cut.

The principal, fearing a lawsuit, relented and pulled the reindeer melody from the show. As you might imagine, this decision led to all sorts of problems. Parents dutifully expressed outrage. School administrators debated, lawyers were consulted, and an all-out investigation of Rudolph was launched to determine whether the red-nosed creature was religious or not.

When all was said and done, the attorneys declared Rudolph was not a religious icon and, therefore, the song could be performed in the holiday show.

I think I need another shot of egg nog.

Town Bans Christmas Cross

For nearly seventy years a cross erected on top of the hose tower at the Central Street Fire Station in Holliston, Massachusetts, served as a beacon of the Christmas season. But that all changed in 2004 when the Holliston Board of Selectmen ordered the cross removed over fears of a lawsuit.

"Signs of the season are fine," Selectmen Chairman Andy Porter told the local newspaper. "But a cross is a symbol of religion versus a symbol of a holiday."[7]

That wasn't good enough for the firefighters who argued that the cross was a cherished tradition within the volunteer department. So over the past few years, firefighter Gregg Lewis said they've been conducting a sort of covert operation—erecting the cross and then taking it down once someone complained.

The firefighters said they are frustrated by the lack of respect for the cross and what it means to the volunteers. "A lot of history, a lot of tradition with the cross," said Lt. Mark Dellicker. "It's been handed down from generation to generation. We feel like we're letting all of the past firefighters down by letting it go. We're not trying to offend anybody, but it means a lot to us."

Scott Foster, the pastor of the town's First Baptist Church, said he's worried that the meaning behind the symbols of the season could get lost in political battles. "I never cease to be surprised at how much controversy comes up over displaying religious symbols," he said, noting it seems Christians are singled out "a little bit more" than other religions.

Christmas Cleansing

Florida Gulf Coast University is giving in to political correctness and banning Christmas decorations. No Santa Claus, no reindeer, and certainly no nativity scenes.

University President Wilson Bradshaw explained why he outlawed Christmas decorations in a memorandum to students and faculty. It reads in part: "Public institutions, including FGCU, often struggle with how best to observe the season in ways that honor and respect all traditions. This is a challenging issue each year at FGCU and 2008 is no exception. While it may appear at times that a vocal majority of opinion is the only view that is held, this is not always the case."

Dr. Bradshaw said his ban was not an attempt to suppress expression of the holiday spirit. On the contrary, it was a *successful* attempt to suppress expression of the holiday spirit. I suspect this doesn't have as much to do with Santa as it does the true meaning of Christmas.

Meanwhile, the lobbies of two libraries at the University of North Carolina are lacking a bit of holiday cheer. The two Christmas trees normally displayed there have been banished, and you can blame it on political correctness.

The Charlotte Observer is reporting librarians censored the display because employees complained. Sarah Michalak, the associate provost for university libraries, told the newspaper: "We strive in our collection to have a wide variety of ideas. It doesn't seem right to celebrate one particular set of customs."[8]

You might recall that UNC is a public university that once required its incoming freshmen to read a book about the Koran. (Ahem.)

Axe the Angel

Angels and stars no longer adorn Christmas trees in Sonoma County, California. And you can thank an aggressive atheist for that. Irv Sutley told his story to *The New York Times*. He was inside a government building when he saw a Christmas tree. "And then," he told the newspaper, "I noticed the angel."[9] He went to another office building and discovered another tree—this one adorned with stars.

"For most people, a star atop a tree at this time of season represents the star of Bethlehem, which is a cult symbol, the cult being Christianity," he said.

Sutley complained, and Sonoma County decided to consult with their lawyers. In the end the county decided government should be neutral on religion, and this resulted in a religious cleansing of Sonoma County's Christmas trees.

Whacking Christmas Bells

The clock tower at Southern Illinois University has played Christmas carols for nearly fifteen years. But this year someone got their bells jingled, and university officials decided to silence the music until they could have a more diverse selection of holiday tunes.

"We got a complaint about not being inclusive in the music," university Chancellor Rita Cheng said. But the rumor around town was the Christmas carols were "religious" and "offensive to non-Christians."

"No one really complained about it being religious," she told FOX News Radio. "They asked that their religion also be reflected in the music."[10]

Cheng said they were specifically asked to include Jewish music, and they may also add some Kwanza tunes.

"That is part of the season," she said. "We have a large number of African-American students at Southern Illinois University, and we would want to be as inclusive as we can."

It's unclear who complained, but Cheng denied the silenced chimes were part of a war on Christmas. "Students who were on the campus from across the world raised the issue, and we're trying to be as responsive as possible and as inclusive," she said. "Christmas is a wonderful time of year, and we don't want to dampen the spirit and the goodwill people have."

But that's exactly what it's done among some students and the Carbondale community. "I miss the Christmas music," student John Piencak told KFVS-TV. "It was really cold, and [when I] walked out of my class to my car and I heard 'Jingle Bells,' it made me happy."[11]

Beth Freeburg works near the clock tower and told WSIL-TV she enjoyed the Christmas music. "I think it's just a wonderful, inspirational thing," she said.

Others, however, suggested the university should strictly play secular holiday tunes.

"If it was 'Jingle Bells' or 'White Christmas' or something like that, I think it would be a lot more respectful,"[12] student Christine Stowell told WSIL-TV.

Another student, Leah Rosenblat, said the change was appropriate. "I think it's awesome. My respect for the university has gone up immensely with its decision to do this."

Chancellor Cheng said the university staff assured her they could add other religious songs to the chimes without taking away from the Christian element.

"On a college campus, I would expect some dialogue," she said. "We just wanted the full campus community to feel included."

Everyone, that is, except the Christians.

No war on Christmas? My friends, the battle has just begun.

16

A Few Moments
with Sean Hannity

 Sean Hannity is living the American dream. He is one of the most popular radio and television hosts in the nation. His books have been best sellers. And he's spoken in sold-out concert halls across the country.

But at his heart Sean is one of us. He's a man who believes in God, loves his family, and loves his country. He grew up in Long Island, New York, in a working-class neighborhood. He knows what it's like to endure hardship. He knows what it means to live from paycheck to paycheck. He understands what it's like to want a better life for his children.

I've met lots of famous folks in New York City, and sometimes what you see on television isn't reality. But Sean is different. He's the real deal. He doesn't walk around town in million-dollar suits. He doesn't have an entourage. And more often than not, you'll find him wearing blue jeans, kicking back with his family, or taking time to raise awareness and support for the fighting men and women of the U.S. Armed Services.

Simply put, Sean is a great American.

Todd: I want to take you back to the 2008 presidential campaign. Then Senator Obama was at an event in San Francisco. He talked about bitter Americans.

Hannity: Clinging to their guns and religion. It's conde-
scending for liberals to think that the American people just
don't get it. John Kerry said the country has entered a period of
know-nothing-ism.

The attacks against the Tea Party Movement and American
citizens have been almost unprecedented. There is a level of outright arrogance that liberals have toward the American people.

But in the 2010 mid-term elections, the American people got
their say, and they spoke loudly. President Obama can say it was a
communications problem all he wants, but when you look at the
exit polls, people got it. They understand that nationalized health
care was rammed down their throats, using backroom deals and
the moral equivalency of bribery to get it passed. Remember the
Cornhusker Kickback? The Louisiana Purchase? It was politics as
usual. President Obama was supposed to be this huge transforma-
tive figure—and transparent on top of that. But he did not deliver
what he promised to the American people.

Todd: Is it just me, or does the White House seem to have a
lack of respect for the traditions and institutions of the country?

Hannity: When President Obama was running for office with
his teleprompter, he had a very disciplined and, frankly, very well-
run campaign. The crowds got excited. He read his teleprompter
with such confidence. I don't think a lot of people even realized he
was reading a teleprompter. But now it's become a national joke.
I wouldn't be surprised if he sleeps with it.

If you want to know Barack Obama, you've got to look into
his background. And we spent a lot of time and took a lot of heat
for going into his radical past, his radical associations.

We looked at his relationship with ACORN and folks like
the Reverend Jeremiah Wright, his pastor for twenty years.
Remember Bill Ayers and Bernadine Dorn? Obama said during
the campaign he was just a guy in the neighborhood. But Obama
started his political career in their home. He sat on boards with an
unrepentant terrorist, gave speeches with the guy, and the media
gave him a pass.

In one moment without a teleprompter, Obama talked about spreading the wealth around. Joe Biden said it was our patriotic duty. This is fundamentally what he thinks America should be, a European socialist state.

Predictably, that kind of state does not lead to opportunity. A socialist state did not create the wealth that is the envy of the world. I believe President Obama has failed in his job. He's failed to get the economy rolling. In spite of all his apology tours, he's failed to gain the respect of the international community, and that was so important to him.

Todd: Liberals say the culture war is over. The conservatives lost on issues like abortion and gay marriage.

Hannity: Why would they say that when every time gay marriage is put on the ballot, it gets rejected? How is that viewed as a loss?

Todd: So you think the nation is still engaged in a culture war?

Hannity: Well, you brought up gay marriage. I think most people do not want to change the definition of marriage, which is evidenced by a number of these referendums that have taken place around this country. Let me say this, since Barack Obama was elected president, I would argue that conservatives have won the arguments.

That's why we had the historic election in 2010. I think conservatives have won. We've won the debate of taxes, and we've won the debate on health care. Most people see President Obama as a socialist, and most people want to reverse course.

Most people want lower taxes; they want the Bush-era tax cuts extended. Most people want Washington to live within its means. They want to cut spending. Exit polls in the 2010 mid-term elections showed most Americans wanted to repeal Obamacare. Most people want to eliminate the death tax. And when they understand what the capital gains tax is, they want the same there.

Todd: Tell me about the phrase "great American."

Hannity: Bill Cunningham, a radio talk-show host from Cincinnati, used that line. He's a friend of mine. When I started my national radio show, every person who called from Cincinnati would say, just like Bill Cunningham did, "You, sir, are a great American! I want a full report."

I'd do it in his voice. Then all of a sudden people just started calling up and saying, "You're a great American, you're a great American, you're a great American." It sort of took on a life of its own. I had to get copyright privileges from Bill Cunningham to let it continue. But it just started out as an inside radio joke with a really good friend of mine.

Todd: But what does it mean to you? What does it mean to be a "great American?"

Hannity: On Election Day in 2010, I went on the air, and I did a long monologue. I spent a lot of time thinking about what I wanted to say. I figured out that what happened on Election Day wasn't about one person. You think of all the people, all the time, all the energy, all the resources that were contributed.

People who were never involved in the political process showed up at town hall meetings. The attended Tea Party events. They weren't seeking fame. They weren't seeking fortune. They just wanted their country to be on a better track. Those are the people who made 2010 happen.

And who are these people? They are the folks who get up every morning, shovel a little coffee down their throats, and then work really hard providing goods and services all day for other people.

They pay their taxes, they obey the laws, they play by the rules, and they make the country a better place. They finally got to a point where they saw the government as intrusive in their daily lives. They're the great Americans.

Todd: Why do you love America?

Hannity: I believe what President Ronald Reagan once said— about that shining city on a hill. I believe the United States of America is the greatest, single-best country God gave man.

I love freedom. I love the idea that you have choices, you take on an individual responsibility in your life. And I contend that you cannot fail in America if you want to succeed.

There is more opportunity for more people in this country than anybody ever dreamed of. We've been able to build up a country full of wealth. I've been to some of the poorest housing projects in America—the Rockaways in New York and the Bronx and Techwood Homes in Atlanta. It's certainly not, in many cases, the ideal place you want to live, but people do have plumbing and running water. They've got televisions and stereos. People have cars and a standard of living that is decent and respectable. But the housing projects give them a platform where they can work really hard and make a better life for themselves.

My father did that. He grew up really poor in Bed-Stuy, a neighborhood in Brooklyn. After he fought four years in the Pacific during World War II, he got a 50-x-100 lot on Long Island, and he created a better standard of living for his family. He was proud of what he accomplished.

My father was standing on the shoulders of his grandfather who came from Ireland. He worked really hard so his family would have a better life in America. And I stand on both their shoulders. The idea here is that if you really work hard in America, great things can happen.

I was eight years old when I started delivering papers. When I was twelve years old, I was scrubbing pots and pans. I was busing tables and waiting tables. By the time I was seventeen, I was tending bar. I did every job imaginable. I was a construction worker. I laid tile, hung wallpaper, painted houses, framed houses. I fell two-and-a-half stories while I was roofing a house.

When I left home and started out on my journey that would lead me into talk radio and eventually to FOX News Channel, I had a thousand dollars in my pocket. I lost $300 when the entire exhaust system fell out of my car.

Do you know that for a long time I never bought a car that cost more than three hundred dollars? I bought an old Providence Gas Company van for $200. It ran on propane. I spent $350 on a Ford Maverick with 168,000 miles on it. I'd fix up those cars. I'd paint them and change the brakes, give them a tune-up.

I was slowly making my way through life, slowly accumu-
lating money. I even went to school—going in and out as I had
the money to pay for it. I never expected anyone else to give me
money or a scholarship.

And then I got behind a radio microphone, and that was it.
It changed me. The minute I got behind that microphone, I knew
that was what I wanted to do.

Todd: You've got it all. You've got a successful career, you've
got money, but at the end of the day, what is the legacy, what is
the one thing you want to leave your kids with, the one thing you
want them to know about life?

Hannity: For me it always comes down to the basics—God,
family, and your country. It's that simple. For anybody to be truly
happy and successful, I think it's predicated on faith and a belief
in God. You've got to appreciate the gifts you have and always
take care of your family.

Living in America is a gift. Not everybody around the world
has the ability to get up and look deep inside themselves, find out
what their dream is, what their skill set is, and then set out with
the odds being very high that they can succeed in creating a living for themselves while providing for other people. That is the
American story.

I want to give my kids the skill set so they can find whatever
gifts God gave them, and then they can share those gifts with
other people. Every person on this earth was born with talent,
natural talent by God, endowed by their Creator.

So if you believe every human soul is endowed by their Creator,
then it's predicated on a belief that they've got talent. When you
live in a free society, you can find it. When you find it, you're going
to be helping humanity, advancing the human condition, while
providing for yourself and your family. That means making a profit.

So that's the best you can expect in life. It doesn't get any
better than that. It's like the Brooks and Dunn song, "That's What
It's All About."[1]

17

Islamophobia Gone Wild

Islamic radicals are coming to town, and I don't believe they're interested in hosting a potluck dinner with the Presbyterians.

"We believe that one day the flag of Islam will fly over the White House," said Muslim cleric Anjem Choudary on ABC's *This Week.* "We do believe as Muslims the East and the West will be governed by Sharia."[1]

From my vantage point it's pretty understandable why Baptists in Alabama might be a bit unsettled with Muslims wanting to build a mosque on Capitol Hill. But liberals have been quick to pounce. They argue that anyone opposed to such things are uneducated, misinformed, and—wait for it—Islamophobic. That's the word they use to describe bitter Americans who have a fear of getting blown up.

But something strange is happening across the country. We're beginning to see bits and pieces of Sharia law incorporated into our national fabric. Some folks might call me an alarmist, but I'm not so sure.

My investigations reveal enough to give me fears that Sharia is indeed creeping across the country, and Muslims are using public schools as an incubator for their brand of religious fundamentalism. They may be banning the Bible, but the nation's public schools are embracing the burka. In New York City schools are allowed to display Islamic symbols, but those of Christian are banned.

"What's at work is the politics of multiculturalism: tolerance for some, intolerance for others," said Bill Donohue, president of the Catholic League.

Across the Hudson River, school officials in South Brunswick, New Jersey, voted to close schools on the Muslim holidays of Ramadan and Eid al-Adha. It's interesting that Christian students are not afforded the same opportunity for their holidays. South Brunswick calls Christmas break "Winter Break." And Easter break is called "Spring Break."

In Dearborn, Michigan, a high school football team moved its preseason practices to 11:00 p.m. to accommodate Muslim players who are not allowed to eat or drink during daylight hours during Ramadan. So the players at Fordson High School held late-night practices that started at 11:00 p.m. and ended at 4:00 a.m. The national media picked up the story and was apparently not able to find one person who objected to a public school revising policy to accommodate the demands of a minority religion.

Could you imagine the media coverage if your neighborhood soccer program was forced to cancel Sunday morning practice to accommodate the local First Baptist Church?

The irony at Fordson High School is that Christians are not afforded the same considerations as Muslims. That's why the school's former wrestling coach filed a federal lawsuit against the Dearborn Public School system and the principal of the high school.

Gerald Marszalek said he was fired after thirty-five years on the job because of his Christian beliefs. According to the Associated Press, Coach Marszalek's troubles began when a volunteer assistant coach introduced Muslim students to Christianity.[2] It didn't seem to matter to school officials that the conversation took place off-campus during a private wrestling camp. The volunteer, who is a minister, lost his job.

Later that year the principal, a devout Muslim, informed the coach that his contract would not be renewed. Coach Marszalek said he was told the issue involved his association with the minister-coach and his religious beliefs.

Meanwhile, a group of Christian missionaries was arrested in Dearborn, accused of disorderly conduct after they tried to share their faith with Muslims attending the annual Arab Fest. The missionaries, some of whom are converted Muslims, were released by police in this heavily Arab suburb of Detroit.

Police Chief Ron Haddad told the Associated Press they are not taking sides, but they are required to keep the peace.[3] In the past, authorities have banned Christians from witnessing at Arab Fest out of safety concerns. One evangelist, George Saieg, filed a lawsuit.

But the issue is not confined just to America. A growing number of public schools across England, for example, are forcing children to eat halal food to accommodate the dietary rules of Muslims.

Parents are absolutely outraged. "We can't force our culture on someone else because that's not right so we shouldn't have someone else's culture forced on us," Jacqueline Gomm told the *Daily Mail*. "The little culture that we have is being lost."[4]

But school officials are standing firm, and Muslim groups claimed that anyone opposed to the rules is guilty of racism.

Did you also know that Muslims and non-Muslims are not allowed to swim in the same pools? That's what David Toube was told when he took his five-year-old son to a public swimming pool north of London. The staff told Toube that he could not swim because he and his son were the wrong religion.

"I arrived at the pool to discover they were holding what staff described to me as 'Muslim men only swimming,'" he wrote online. "I was told that the session was for Muslims only and that we could not be admitted."

According to the *Daily Mail*, the staff informed Mr. Toube they would only be allowed inside the public swimming pool if the Muslims didn't object.[5]

And that's not all. I submit for you even more examples of "Islamaphobia Gone Wild" from the fly-over states.

High School Tests Slam Christianity

A state-mandated test administered to high school students across New York portrayed Islam as a religion of peace and Christianity as a religion of violence. The bias was so blatant a number of teachers complained to state officials.

"There should have been a little balance in there," one teacher told the *New York Post*. "To me, this was offensive because it's so inappropriate."[6]

State education leaders said they made every effort to make sure all religions were presented accurately.

But that did not happen. Check out this excerpt from the reading portion of the exam republished in the *Post*: "Wherever they went, the Moslems (sic) brought with them their love of art, beauty and learning. From about the eighth to eleventh century, their culture was superior in many ways to that of western Christendom."

Now read what the test had to say about Christian missionaries in Latin America: "Idols, temples and other material evidences of paganism [were] destroyed," and "Christian buildings [were] often constructed on sites of destroyed native temples."

Sixth-Graders Pray to Allah on Field Trip

A group of public schoolchildren were separated by gender and allowed to participate in midday prayers during a field trip to a Boston-area mosque, and now the school is apologizing.

Attorney Rob Meltzer said the incident allegedly occurred when a social studies class from Wellesley Middle School toured the Islamic Society of Boston Cultural Center, one of the largest mosques in the Northeast.

His client was a chaperone on the trip and videotaped the

events. The video was distributed by Americans for Peace and Tolerance, a religious advocacy group that has been critical of the Boston mosque.

Parents were told their children would be learning about the architecture of a mosque, and they would be allowed to observe a prayer service. However, the students were in fact given a lecture on the Prophet Mohammed, and some male students participated in a midday prayer service.

"You have to believe in Allah, and Allah is the one God, the only one worthy of worship, all forgiving, all merciful," a mosque spokesperson reportedly told the students.

"Personally, I was appalled," Meltzer told me. "We are obviously very concerned about how much control parents were given and the lack of informed consent."

The sixth-graders were also allegedly told *jihad* is a personal spiritual struggle and has nothing to do with holy war. Female students were told Islam is a pro-women's religion.

"Islam was actually very advanced in terms of recognizing women's rights," said an unidentified mosque spokesperson in the video. "At the time of the Prophet Mohammed, women were allowed to express their opinions and vote. In this country women didn't gain that right until less than a hundred years ago."

The students were then instructed on how to pray during the midday service.

Mosque officials separated the group by gender and invited male students to join traditional Muslim prayers. The video shows young boys bowing and prostrating themselves with their heads touching the floor.

Dennis Hale, a spokesman for Americans for Peace and Tolerance, said the incident illustrates how the mosque was engaged in proselytizing. "You can easily imagine what would have happened if a Catholic priest had taken some kids from a school to teach them about Catholicism and have them take Communion without telling the parents," he said. "The furor would be visible from outer space."

At no point during the event did any schoolteacher or school official intervene. But nearly four months later, when the incident finally became known, the Wellesley School District sent a letter to parents apologizing for what happened.

"I extend my sincere apologies for the error that occurred and regret the offense it may have caused," wrote Superintendent Bella Wong in a statement provided to me. "In the future, teachers will provide more clear guidance to students to better define what is allowed to fulfill the purpose of observation."

Wong explained the field trip was part of a course titled "Enduring Beliefs and the World Today." It included a visit to a synagogue and a mosque along with a gospel music concert and meeting with representatives of the Hindu religion.

Wong admitted that five students participated in the midday Muslim prayers. She also confirmed that a parent videotaped the incident.

"It was not the intent for students to be able to participate in any of the religious practices," she wrote. "The fact that any students were allowed to do so in this case was an error."

Cop Demoted for Refusing to Attend Muslim Prayers

The Tulsa Police Department is investigating a captain who refused an order to assign officers to attend an upcoming Islamic event because he said it would violate his religious beliefs.

Captain Paul Fields was reassigned after he refused to order officers under his command to attend the Islamic Center of Tulsa's Law Enforcement Appreciation Day, a spokesman for the department said. "It is my opinion and that of my legal counsel that forcing me to enter a Mosque when it is not directly related to a police call for service is a violation of my civil rights," Fields wrote in an internal police department memo obtained by FOX News.[7]

"I have no problem with officers attending on a voluntary basis; however, I take exception to requiring officers to attend this event," Fields wrote in an e-mail obtained by FOX News to his superior officer. "I believe this directive to be an unlawful order, as it is in direct conflict with my personal religious convictions."

"When you become a police officer, you don't give up any of your constitutional rights," said Scott Wood, an attorney representing Fields.

The lawsuit named Deputy Chief Daryl Webster as the lone defendant, accusing him of retaliating against Fields for exercising his First Amendment rights.

Fields has been on the police force for sixteen years and has at least six commendations. Wood says Fields has had a "stellar career" without any disciplinary actions.

In essence, Wood said Field was retaliated against for not voluntarily attending a mosque. It's a case of political correctness, he said.

"That's definitely what it is," Wood said. "But political correctness has nothing to do with the First Amendment."

The events leading to the lawsuit started when members of the Tulsa Police Department were invited to attend a "Law Enforcement Appreciation Day" at the Islamic Center of Tulsa. It was advertised as a social gathering featuring food, an opportunity to watch a Muslim prayer service, and an invitation to join lectures on beliefs, human rights, and women.

According to Wood, no one responded to the invitations, and no one volunteered. The following day Fields received a directive ordering him to find officers to attend.

"This is a program put on by the mosque for the officers, not the officers for the mosque," Wood said. "He did not believe it was police-related or related to his duties, and he was not going to do something that conflicted with his religious beliefs."

Wood said to their knowledge Tulsa police officers have never been ordered to attend nonpolice-related events at synagogues or Christian houses of worship.

The controversy has sparked national interest among Muslims. Ibrahim Hooper, the spokesman for the Council on

America-Islamic Relations said he was following the incident and said it's an example of "anti-Muslim bigotry. When somebody feels empowered to say, 'I'm not going to take part in a community outreach event at a mosque because I basically don't like Muslims,' it's all part of that rise in Islamophobia in our society," he said.

But Scott emphatically denied CAIR's accusations. "Captain Fields would lay down his life for anyone in that mosque if the need arose regardless of their color, creed, or background," Wood said. "The purported reason for this law-enforcement appreciation day was because of the department's performance in catching someone who had made threats against the mosque. You can't have it both ways. 'You did a great job protecting us, but you're a bigot?'"

Muslims Told to Stay Away from FBI

The Council on American Islamic Relations featured a poster on its Web site promoting an upcoming conference that encourages people not to talk to the Federal Bureau of Investigation. The poster, which appeared on the Web site of CAIR's California chapter, features a sinister-looking FBI agent with the headlines, "Build a Wall of Resistance" and "Don't Talk to the FBI."

"I think it's subject to misinterpretation," spokesman Ibrahim Hooper told me.

Although it seems pretty clear to me.

The poster was promoting a conference called "FBI Raids and Grand Jury Subpoenas: Know Your Rights and Defend Our Communities." The keynote speaker was Hatem Abudayyeh, identified by CAIR as an activist and Palestinian community leader whose home was allegedly raided by federal agents.

Hooper conceded the poster "crosses the line" but refused to renounce the artwork and blamed critics for fomenting what he called a manufactured controversy. "The entire American-Muslim community is under the microscope right now with a cottage industry of Muslim bashers," he said. "We're used to this kind of attack by the Islamophobic hate machine, and in this case there is some justification in terms of the possibility of misinterpretation of this poster."

Former FBI assistant director Bill Gavin told me the poster is sending the wrong message to the Muslim community.

"It sends out a real negative attitude to the Islamic community of what the FBI is really all about," Gavin said. "This is just a propaganda tool to try and thwart an active investigation into criminal acts by a would-be terrorist group.

"Why wouldn't you talk to the FBI?" Gavin wondered. "If in fact there is something being done to destroy the image of Islam in the United States, then it should be stopped. We should put a positive face on Islam, not Islamic extremists."

Remember the story of the frog and the pot of boiling water? If you put the frog into the water before it starts to boil, the frog will never get out. And by the time the frog realizes what's going on, it's too late.

Friends, if radical Islam is the pot, America may be ready to croak.

Sex Tents, Gerbils, and San Francisco Values

It appears the folks in San Francisco have been smoking too much granola. In 2010 the city outlawed the sale of Coca-Cola, considered a ban on the sale of pets, and contemplated pitching public sex tents so folks can do what comes unnaturally in front of God, country, and presumably kindergartners.

The debate over the sex tents involves the city's Folsom Street Fair. Apparently a few people were understandably offended at the forthright fornication coinciding with this event, even with the well-known nature of the gathering and the sordid reputation of its provocative participants. But after dutifully notifying the police of their shock and concern, they were told that this was San Francisco, where "the unwritten rule for the fair was, live and let live."[1]

However, one complaint led to further complaints, and eventually a meeting was called to discuss the issue. That's where they came up with the idea of public sex tents. As the newspaper noted, folks could have sex there or just watch.

Supervisor Beven Dufty represents the Castro district. He's in favor of the tents, or at least in favor of exploring the idea.

"There are definitely people interested in seeing more public sex," Dufty told *The Bay Area Reporter.* "Right now, I'd just take it under advisement and wait and see what develops."

Tell me I didn't just hear that. From a government official.

Now most folks in the fly-over states would agree that what people do in their bedroom is their own business. But what you do in a pup tent over by the monkey bars is a totally different matter. The proposal caused even the liberals over at the *San Francisco Chronicle* to choke on their tofu.

"Public sex isn't just lewd; it's illegal under state law," opined the newspaper's editorial board. "Enough. This is a quality of life issue that should have been tackled years ago. Local leaders need to stop clowning around and insist that everyone obey the law."[2]

Meanwhile, another crisis is developing at City Hall where they've banned soft drinks. Mayor Gavin Newsome has issued an executive order banning Coke, Pepsi, and Fanta Orange from vending machines on city property. The directive also includes nondiet sodas, sports drinks, and artificially sweetened water. That means if you need to wash down that tofu turkey dog, you'll need to order a bottle of soy milk. Even fruit juices have come under the mayor's scrutiny. Juices must be made from 100 percent juice with no added sweeteners.

So what's a thirsty San Franciscan supposed to drink?

Well, according to the mayor, the city's vending machines will be stocked with a wide variety of "healthy" alternatives. Imagine nursing a glass of rice milk on a warm, sunny day. The machines will also be stocked with water, provided it meets fat and sugar content requirements.

According to the *San Francisco Chronicle*, the ban is part of the mayor's effort to slim the city's waistlines. "There's a direct link between what people eat and drink and the obesity and health care crisis in this country," Newsom spokesman Tony Winnicker told the newspaper. "It's entirely appropriate and not at all intrusive for city government to take steps to discourage the sale of sugary sodas on city property."[3]

Not intrusive unless, of course, you want a bottle of root beer or a Fresca.

The city's ban is believed to be one of the strictest in the nation, and it's drawn the ire of the California/Nevada Soft Drink Association.

"This is all about choice," Executive Director Bob Achermann told the *Chronicle*. "There is probably nothing more personal than what you drink or eat. Singling out beverages in this whole equation of how to fight obesity is not going to be the answer."

But Winnicker said the only thing they are banning is the *sale* of soft drinks, not the actual consumption. "People absolutely remain free to choose to drink unhealthy sugary sodas anywhere they want," he told the newspaper. "Selling them is another matter."

Now if that doesn't curdle your wheatgrass smoothie, wait until you hear about the proposed ban on house pets.

The city's Commission of Animal Control and Welfare is considering an ordinance that would make it a crime to sell pets— including dogs, cats, gerbils, hamsters, mice, rats—everything except fish.

If the ordinance is passed, San Francisco could become the first city in the nation to ban the sale of all pets.

"People buy small animals all the time as an impulse buy, don't know what they're getting into, and the animals end up at the shelter and often are euthanized," Chairwoman Sally Stephens told the *Chronicle*. "That's what we'd like to stop."[4]

But others, including the Pet Industry Joint Advisory Board, suspect there's another motive.

"This is an anti-pet proposal from people who oppose the keeping of pets," said Michael Maddox, the general counsel for the group. "If their goal is to ban the ownership of pets entirely, then this is a good first step."

Pet store owners are fighting mad.

"It's terrible," pet store manager John Chan told the newspaper. "A pet store that can't sell pets? It's ridiculous."

It's almost as ridiculous as banning Mr. Pibb from city hall.

19

The War on the Boy Scouts

 I was a Cub Scout. I promised to do my best, do my duty to God and my country, help other people, and obey the law of the pack. I remember how proud I felt on den meeting day when I wore my uniform to school, walking the hallways of Hope P. Sullivan Elementary School in my royal blue shirt and bright yellow neckerchief.

I learned how to tie knots, build campfires, and pick up trash along the back roads of north Mississippi. But my career as a Scout came to a rather abrupt end during a Fourth of July parade. Our den was invited to ride along on a float and toss out candy along the parade route.

I was having the time of my life until the tractor hauling our float jolted to a stop. The peppermints flew off in one direction, and I flew off in the other. My bottom and my ego were thoroughly bruised, and I decided my career as a Scout was over.

Nevertheless, I've always had deep respect for the Boy Scouts of America. These young men represent the best of America. They aspire to serve God and their country, putting others ahead of themselves.

I speak of Eagle Scouts like Jacob Chavez, of Austin, Texas. He was hanging out with a friend at an apartment complex when a two-year-old child was pulled out of a swimming pool. Jacob immediately went to work, administering CPR until paramedics arrived. As a result of his quick action, the boy survived.

On Super Bowl Sunday, Cub Scout Germainye Hudson saved his grandmother's life. He was at a party when Bernadette Hudson began choking. The fifth-grader from Crestview, Florida, performed the Heimlich maneuver.

"Every time I look at Germainye, I know he's the reason I'm here," Mrs. Hudson told the local newspaper. "I'm very proud of him."[1]

And then there's the story of Edward Myers, a Boy Scout from Greensboro, North Carolina. He was planting trees in a park when he discovered a purse. Inside the purse was $2,000 in cash.

"I was shocked," he told local television station WGHP-TV. "I mean, seeing this much money, it was unbelievable."[2]

What was even more unbelievable is what happened next. The eleven-year-old Boy Scout called the police and handed over the purse. When the rightful owner claimed her money, she gave Edward a hundred dollars.

"You know, I wouldn't care if she gave me a reward," he said. "I felt good (about) what I did."

And there are dozens, if not hundreds, of similar stories about Boy Scouts going the extra mile, doing the right thing, performing random acts of kindness. But sadly this uniquely American institution is under attack. The values they cling to—allegiance to God, allegiance to country, and a promise to help others—are being assaulted by liberals, Democrats, and even public service unions. Some, in effect, have declared war on the Scouts.

California Democrats Bash Scouts

Democrats in California's Assembly killed a proposal to honor the Boy Scouts of America as they commemorated their one hundredth anniversary. The proposed resolution died in the Assembly Judiciary Committee on a party-line vote.

According to the *Los Angeles Times*, Committee Chairman

Mike Feuer led the opposition, "citing the Scout's history of not allowing gays to serve in their leadership."[3]

Republican Assemblyman Curt Hagman, a former Eagle Scout, called the Democrats' action "kind of crazy." "With all the resolutions we do here, they're not all perfect," Hagman told the *Times*. "If you don't support it, just [don't vote for] it, but to oppose the Boy Scouts on their birthday seems silly."

He's not the only one. California's Republican Party chairman, Ron Nehring, issued a statement condemning the Democrats. "I guess if you're trustworthy, loyal, helpful, friendly, courteous, kind, obedient, cheerful, thrifty, brave, clean, and reverent, there appears to be little room for you in the California Democratic Party," he said in a written statement.

I believe he just may have a point.

A Subversive Group?

The enemy was dangerous, subversive, and the Pentagon warned military bases around the world to be extremely careful. Was this despicable force al Qaeda? Nope. Were they domestic terrorists? Not even close. The subversive foe was the Boy Scouts of America.

In 2004 the Pentagon directed military bases not to directly sponsor Boy Scout troops because the organization banned openly gay scout leaders. But that wasn't the real issue. It seems as though the Scouts are required to swear an oath of duty to God, and this is what had the Pentagon brass shaking in their boots.

The Pentagon's directive was part of a settlement reached between the military and civil liberties advocates, specifically the ACLU.

"If our Constitution's promise of religious liberty is to be a reality, the government should not be administering religious oaths or discriminating based on religious beliefs,"[4] said ACLU attorney Adam Schwartz in an interview with the Associated Press.

Service members are still allowed to lead Scout troops but only in an unofficial capacity. And their participation must be strictly on their own time.

The ACLU, however, isn't finished with their attacks on the Scouts. They want the military to defund all Scouting events. The military reportedly spends several million dollars annually to host the Boy Scout Jamboree. The Defense Department also provides financial support for Boy Scout units on military bases overseas.

The battle lines have been drawn—accept homosexuals and reject God.[5] We know which side the ACLU is on. I'm beginning to wonder which side the Pentagon is on.

A Not-So-Gay Parade

Homosexuals are on the warpath in Vermont. They want state lawmakers to defund the annual Veteran's Day Parade because it's hosted by the Boy Scouts. The gay-rights crowd said the Scouts should not receive a dime of state money because the group is "discriminatory."

"I personally do not believe we should use taxpayer dollars to support organizations that aren't inclusive of all of Vermont's citizens,"[6] Senate President Peter Shumlin told the newspaper. "To have state taxpayer money support an organization with anti-gay policies is deeply disturbing, particularly at a time when we're seeing so many funding cuts to our most vulnerable residents,"[7] said Kara DeLeonardis in an interview with the *Times Argus* newspaper.

We're not talking about a lot of money, folks—about $7,500—but the homosexuals remain adamantly opposed, even if it means cancelling the state's annual Veteran's Day Parade.

"If it wasn't for the money in the governor's budget, we wouldn't be able to host the parade," said Rick Stockton, head of the governing body of the Vermont Boy Scouts, adding that children are allowed to join the Scouts regardless of sexual orientation.

However, the Boy Scouts strictly forbid openly gay or lesbian *adults* from volunteering as troop leaders, supported by a 2000 U.S. Supreme Court ruling. And that's the bur under the opposition's saddle. As you might imagine, the American Civil Liberties Union also weighed in, throwing their support behind the anti-Scouts crowd.

All of which throws rainwater on the Veteran's Day parade in Vermont.

Union Leader Calls for Investigation of Scouts

Kevin Anderson just wanted to earn his Eagle Scout badge. Instead, he's come under fire from Allentown, Pennsylvania's biggest union boss who wants to investigate the underage do-gooder after he unknowingly ruffled union feathers.

Anderson has logged in more than two hundred hours to clear a one-thousand-foot walking path along the Lehigh River. "I decided to do my part in completing this part of the trail," he told *The Morning Call* newspaper. "In that way, others could enjoy walking along the river."[8]

But his good deed has drawn fire from the Service Employees International Union. President Nick Balzano threatened to investigate the seventeen-year-old high school junior.

"We'll be looking into the Cub Scout or Boy Scout who did the trails," he reportedly said to the city council.

Last July the city decided to lay off thirty-nine union members who work in the Public Works and Parks and Recreation departments. The young Boy Scout was doing work typically handled by union employees.

City Hall has decided to step into the fray as the teenager faces the wrath of a scorned union. "We would hope that the well-intentioned efforts of an Eagle Scout candidate would not be challenged by the union," Mayor Ed Pawlowski wrote in an e-mail to the local newspaper. "This young man is performing a great service to the community."

The union boss said he's not targeting the Boy Scouts and stressed that it's not personal. Nevertheless, he's playing hardball.

"No one except union members may pick up a hoe or shovel, plant a flower, or clear a walking path," Balzano said.

In other words, the only legal hoe is a union hoe.

Why Can't a Man Be More like a Man?

My fellow Americans, we have a serious problem. Men have started to grow lady parts.

It started in the 1990s, but now we have an entire generation of American men who've lost their manhood. The clinical term is "metrosexual." But Uncle Jerry, from Mississippi, calls them girly-men.

The word *metrosexual* originated in a 1994 article that appeared in *The Independent*.[1] The metrosexual man was defined as "the single young man with a high disposable income, living or working in the city (because that's where all the best shops are) . . . perhaps the most promising consumer market of the decade. In the eighties he was only to be found inside fashion magazines such as GQ, in television advertisements for Levis jeans or in gay bars. In the nineties, he's everywhere and he's going shopping."

In the hit Broadway musical *My Fair Lady*, Professor Henry Higgins laments in a song, "Why can't a woman be more like a man?"[2] Well, it seems Professor Higgins got his wish.

Today's men are more likely to get facial peels and carry man bags. They hire fashion consultants and life coaches. And many guys have started getting in touch with their feelings.

Men's magazines are filled with articles like "Should a Man Show Nipple?" and "What Men Know About Wearing Eyeliner."[3] One men's journal actually encouraged guys to shave their entire bodies. They provided a nine-point checklist for the hairless body, suggesting that one advantage to having denuded legs is that it cuts down on friction. (I say it also makes you look like a terminally ill cat.)

According to Askmen.com, 20 percent of men surveyed have no problem wearing makeup.[4] Can you imagine John Wayne using moisturizer and a concealer stick to hide razor nicks? Would today's version of *The Godfather* accessorize with Dolche Gabana while settling "family" business with group hugs?

The country music industry has been especially hit hard by this trend. In the old days country music crooners used to be Southern rednecks who drank beer, got into bar fights, and wrote love songs from the comfort of their double-wide trailer. Nowadays they sip Shirley Temples, style their hair, and write ballads from their cabanas on South Beach. And their red necks are courtesy of a spray-on tan.

It's so bad we've even had to outsource our superheroes. Hollywood is releasing new films featuring Batman, Spider-Man, and Superman. All three characters are being portrayed by British actors.

I suppose it could have been worse. Can you imagine a French Superman? "Look! Up in the sky! It's a bird, it's a plane. No, it's Le Surhomme! Sacre bleu."

I believe the slippery slope to metrosexualism began when guys stopped getting their hair cut and started getting their hair styled. They stopped going to barber shops and started going to salons.

Back in the old days the barber used to ask you about batting averages and fishing. These days stylists will ask you what kind of "product" you put in your hair.

It's not uncommon to see fellows walking around New York City wearing "guy-liner" with a man bag draped over their shoulder so they can haul around malnourished effete dogs dressed in designer sweaters.

And then, there's the skinny jeans crowd. "I've started to see a lot of men wearing women's skinny jeans, which is barely acceptable if you're twenty-two and crackhead thin," said Dan Peres, editor of *Details* magazine. "I suggest New York men keep their feminine fashion instincts where they belong—in the closet."[5]

Some of the girls in the office suggested I update my look by getting some skinny jeans. It took a shoehorn and a bottle of cooking oil to get me into a pair of those things. Let's just agree that you should only wear skinny jeans if you are in fact skinny.

There is a spiritual component to this issue, according to Randy Stinson. He's the president of the Council on Biblical Manhood and Womanhood. He believes society has created a generation of young men who are the "most self-absorbed generation in American history."

"We are raising our young boys to be way too soft, way too careful, as if the ultimate prize in our parenting of boys is to get them to 18 years old and say they never got hurt, nothing bad ever happened," he said at a conference held at Southern Baptist Theological Seminary. "They never experienced disappointment. They have just had a wonderfully smooth life. What you've done, you have handicapped that boy for the rest of his life. He will be a weak, soft, ineffective man."

The Associated Baptist Press reported on the conference and highlighted Stinson's assertion that male skin-care products and hair products would have been unthinkable a generation ago.[6]

In part, Stinson blamed the "feminization" of the Gospels for the plight that has befallen men, specifically Christian men. "When we talk about the Christian life in terms of sensual, romantic language, why are we surprised when men don't get that and men are repulsed by that? They don't understand that.

"Part of the problem in our church today is that men have this view of Jesus that comes from our Sunday school literature," he said. "His hair is perfectly flowing. His beard is very nice. His skin is smooth." But Stinson said that's not an accurate portrait of Jesus. "He was the son of a carpenter without any power tools, and he walked everywhere in the blistering sun," refuting the idea Jesus looked "womanly and feminine."

He said it's time for Christian men to reclaim their position of spiritual leadership. And the unscientific poll I conducted among a group of female friends seems to suggest he's right on the money.

According to my poll, ladies want a man who loves God and loves his family. They also want a man who, in no particular order:

1. Has a job.
2. Drives a pickup truck.
3. Uses the bathroom standing up.
4. Eats meat.
5. And is willing to carry them out of a burning building.

And nine out of ten ladies said they want a man who would not be caught dead watching Oprah.

Meanwhile, there are signs that manly men are beginning to make a comeback. Women would prefer to watch Tom Selleck than Tom Cruise. And there have been published reports that actor Matthew McConaughey has decided to forgo soap, choosing instead to stew in his own natural aroma. From what I've heard, it's pungent.

And closer to home, Luke, the-sixteen-year-old, has joined a group on Facebook called, "I'm a man, you're a woman—go make me a sandwich."

In an unrelated matter, he seems to be having difficulties finding a date for the prom.

Why Is Daddy Wearing a Dress?

Welcome to the United States of America—where the men are women, the women are men, and the rest of us are just plain confused.

As we take these early steps into the twenty-first century, there are growing signs we may be moving into an age of a genderless society. In the coming years you can expect the words "gender neutral," "gender variant," and "gender queer" to be added to our culture war lexicon. They've even got a pronoun lined up for us to use—"ze"—as in "Ze is neither he nor she."

It's part of a growing movement some are likening to the early days of the gay-rights movement—men and women who consider themselves neither male nor female. The movement has already taken hold on many college and university campuses across the country. Harvard University, Rutgers University, and the University of Michigan are just some of the schools now with gender-neutral housing and unisex bathrooms.

Newsweek addressed the issue in a story titled "Are We Facing a Genderless Future?"[1] Dr. Jack Drescher, a member of the American Psychiatric Association, attempted to answer the question. "There is no way that six billion people can be categorized into two groups," he said. "We don't want to force people to fit into a doctor's categories."

Who knew so many people were confused about this? When I was in grade school, it was pretty easy to figure out which team everyone was on. And anyone who was still confused was ordered to watch the entire first season of *The Dukes of Hazzard*. Daisy Duke had tremendous influence on the males of my generation.

Honestly, folks, I just don't know what to make of the coming genderless society. I long for the old days when God handled the business of creating man in His image. Those were grand times, weren't they? God created our "inward parts," is how the Bible describes it. He knit us together in our mothers' wombs. We were "remarkably and wonderfully made."

But this is the twenty-first century, and mankind has decided they know how to improve the product. Between you and me, I'd love to be a fly on the wall at the pearly gates on rapture day when all these folks have to explain why they've got extra parts the original models didn't have.

Here's a sampling of some early battles in the quest for a genderless society.

Genderless Passports Considered

The State Department briefly considered replacing the words "mother" and "father" on U.S. passport applications with more gender neutral terminology. "The words in the old form were 'mother' and 'father,'" said Brenda Sprague, deputy assistant secretary of state for Passport Services. "They are now 'parent one' and 'parent two.'"[2]

A statement on the State Department Web site noted: "These improvements are being made to provide a gender neutral description of a child's parents and in recognition of different types of families." The statement didn't note if it was for child applications only.

Sprague said the decision to remove the traditional parenting names was not an act of political correctness. "We find, with changes in medical science and reproductive technology, that we are confronting situations now that we would not have anticipated ten or fifteen years ago," she said.

Gay-rights groups are applauding the decision. "Changing the terms *mother* and *father* to the more global term of *parent* allows many different types of families to apply for a passport for their child without feeling like the government doesn't recognize their family," said Jennifer Chrisler, executive director of Family Equality Council.

Her organization lobbied the government for several years to remove the words from passport applications. "Our government needs to recognize that the family structure is changing," Chrisler said. "The best thing we can do is support people who are raising kids in loving, stable families."

But some conservative Christians are outraged over the decision. "Only in the topsy-turvy world of left-wing political correctness could it be considered an 'improvement' for a birth-related document to provide less information about the circumstances of that birth," Family Research Council President Tony Perkins told me. "This is clearly designed to advance the causes of same-sex 'marriage' and homosexual parenting without statutory authority, and it violates the spirit if not the letter of the Defense of Marriage Act."

Robert Jeffress, pastor of First Baptist Church in Dallas, agreed. "It's part of an overall attempt at political correctness to diminish the distinction between men and women and to somehow suggest you don't need both a father and a mother to raise a child successfully," said Jeffress. "[This decision] was made to help homosexual couples feel more comfortable in rearing children."

Chrisler recounted the day she and her female partner tried to get passports for her twin sons.

"Even though my partner was their legal mother, had adopted them after I gave birth to them, she still had to put her name in the father field, and that is both discriminatory and makes us feel like second-class citizens," she said.

Passport Services official Sprague said she would not use the word *discriminatory* to describe the old form. "I would prefer to use the word *imprecise*," she said. "It just didn't capture the reality of their situation. Clearly, we want to be sensitive to the feelings of other people, but we are also conscious of our need to introduce the greatest degree of precision to the process."

Perkins, meanwhile, accused the State Department of disrespecting the law and called on Congress to "take their oversight role very seriously" and to intervene in these circumstances.

Obama Touts Gay Fathers

President Obama saluted gay fathers in his annual Father's Day proclamation—a move that is believed to be a first in presidential history. "Nurturing families come in many forms, and children may be raised by a father and mother, a single father, two fathers, a stepfather, a grandfather, or caring guardian," the president wrote. "For the character they build, the doors they open, and the love they provide over our lifetimes, all our fathers deserve our unending appreciation and admiration."

As noted in *The Washington Post*, it may be the first time gay fathers have been included in a presidential Father's Day proclamation. "George W. Bush's final proclamation in 2008 noted the 'extraordinary effort of the nation's fathers, stepfathers, grandfathers, and guardians,'[3] wrote Alec MacGillis of the *Post*. "And the furthest Obama's proclamation went last year in giving a nod to nontraditional fathering was to 'honor those surrogate fathers who raise, mentor, or care for someone else's child.'"

The move has been heralded in pro-gay Web sites and blogs. GLTNewsnow.com said President Obama was being "all inclusive."

"Glad you recognize that fathers, including gay fathers, not only carry enormous responsibilities, but often serve as mentors, tutors, and leaders within our neighborhoods and communities,"[4] wrote Michael Jones, an editor at Change.org.

The proclamation has not been well received among Christian conservatives, however. "The only two fathers in a home should be God and dad," said Michael Linton, pastor of Hope Fellowship in Humble, Texas. "Unfortunately, it's an even more blatant (if possible) acceptance and endorsement of the homosexual lifestyle than we have previously seen from him.

"It should go without saying that same-sex parents are completely and totally unbiblical," Pastor Linton said. "But here we have the president endorsing a nonbiblical, nontraditional, mostly unaccepted lifestyle by proclamation."

Southern Baptist pastor Mark Wood said conservatives should be upset. "Rightfully so, our country is slipping," he told me. "Even churches are tolerating the unthinkable. This is a prime example of the loss of a standard—the Bible."

School Orders Boys to Dress like Girls

An elementary school in Burlington County, New Jersey, is under fire after ordering boys to dress up in female clothing to celebrate Women's History Month. The activity was eventually cancelled after a number of parents complained to the Maple Shade School District. The cross-dressing day at Maude Wilkins Elementary School was scheduled for April 16, which happens to be the national "Day of Silence," created by a gay advocacy group to bring awareness to anti-bullying efforts.

"All students must participate in the activity," stated a note sent home with students and eventually published online. "If your child is a young man, he does not have to wear a dress or skirt, as there are many time periods where women wore pants or trousers."[5]

Some parents, like Janine Patterson Giandomenico, were outraged. "Asking my nine-year-old son to dress like a woman in a school fashion show in front of his peers is crossing the line for me," she wrote on her Facebook page. "How is dressing like a woman from any era going to teach him about history? I resent the fact that the Maple Shade School District is telling me that he and I have no choice," she wrote.

Superintendent Michael Livengood told me the event was cancelled because it "caused quite a bit of controversy."

"I wish that initial letter had been worded differently," he said. "That was the mistake in the whole process."

Livengood said it was never the principal's intent for the boys to wear skirts. "I understand both sides when you read the letter," he said. "It does say everyone must participate. It does say everyone must wear women's clothing, but that was not the intent."

Livengood said no one at the school is in trouble although he said he probably will remind teachers to be more careful how future letters are worded.

As for the cross-dressing event being scheduled on the same day as the "Day of Silence," Livengood said it was "purely coincidental."

Potty Parity

If the Maine Human Rights Commission has its way, transgendered students would be allowed to choose the bathrooms, locker rooms, and sports teams of their choice. The commission's attorney believes forcing a little girl to use the "little girl's room" is not only unconstitutional—it's illegal.

"Schools cannot discriminate against sexual identity or gender identification," said John Gause, the legal counsel for Maine's Human Rights Commission, in remarks published by WorldNetDaily. "Schools cannot segregate students based on sexual orientation and identity."[6] He suggested that forcing students to use "biology based" restrooms is illegal and must be stopped.

According to an account published in the *Bangor Daily News*, the discussion centered around a document created by the commission called "Sexual Orientation in Schools and Colleges."[7] The document recommends schools let transgender students use bathrooms, play on sports teams, and follow the dress codes of the gender they identify with.

This discussion comes after an incident last summer in which the commission ruled that the Orono School District discriminated against a boy who was denied access to the girl's bathroom. A review of that decision is pending before a state superior court judge.

"This is a commission that exists to protect the human rights of the people of Maine," said Zachary Heidin, of the Maine Civil Liberties Union in an interview with the *Bangor Daily News*. "Maine law protects people from discrimination based on gender identity and expression. Allowing people who are transgender to use the bathroom, which is a basic human need, is entirely consistent with basic human rights as well as Maine law."

Rev. Bob Celeste attended the public hearing but was not allowed to speak. He's opposed to the plan. "All they're interested in doing is using anything as a guise to introduce the children of Maine to the homosexual lifestyle," he told the newspaper.

The commission has already ruled that a middle school discriminated against a sixth-grader by not letting the child, who is a boy, use the girls' bathroom. They're facing a similar struggle in Houston where men who believe they are women can now use the ladies' room.

Mayor Annise Parker signed executive orders prohibiting city workers from harassment or discrimination in hiring, promotion, and contracting based on gender identity, according to the *Houston Chronicle*.[8] The order also allows transgendered people to use restroom facilities in city-owned buildings for the gender with which they identify.

Parker, who is gay, is earning praise from supporters in the gay community. "The mayor wanted to put in writing what has already been the city's practice, which is that we do not discriminate," spokesperson Janice Evans told the newspaper.

The executive orders only impact city workers and not the general public.

"This is essential," said Kris Banks, president of the Houston Gay, Lesbian, Bisexual, and Transgender Political Caucus, in an interview with the *Chronicle*. "A nondiscrimination provision that protects sexual orientation but doesn't protect gender identity is toothless. . . . It's quite a thing, having a mayor that really understands all these issues."

However, the Houston Area Pastors Council is outraged. Critics like Dave Wilson have been labeled "anti-gay." He opposes the mayor's decision.

"Forcing women in particular using city facilities to be subjected to cross-dressing men invading their privacy is beyond the pale and offensive to every standard of decency,"[9] Pastor Steve Riggle told *The Christian Post*.

Herman Castano, who pastors a Hispanic congregation, called the mayor's decision "morally wrong, irresponsible, and indefensible."

But while the experts debate the philosophical and psychological issues involved in the coming genderless society, I have a more practical question to pose in relation to the new genderless bathrooms popping up around the country:

Do you leave the seat up or down?

22

Save Mankind, Eat an Animal

 In the beginning God created the heavens and the earth. He made cows for cheeseburgers, turkeys for Thanksgiving, and chickens for the Baptists.

But somehow over the past few thousand years, mankind has slowly lost its place in the food chain. And now the animal kingdom is getting restless. In fact, it may be only a matter of time before Fluffy satisfies his hunger with something other than Meow Mix.

Consider the following:

In Florida, a naked crackhead was nearly eaten alive by an alligator. As Sheriff Grady Judd so eloquently told FOX News Channel, just because you are a naked crackhead does not give an alligator the right to eat you alive.[1]

In California, there's the horrific story of James Davis, who along with his wife, owned an animal sanctuary where they kept their pet chimpanzee, Moe. One year they decided to throw a birthday bash for their chimp, complete with a cake. So how did Moe decide to celebrate? He attacked Mr. Davis and tore off his testicles.

But the most egregious example of animal-on-human violence happened in 2010 at Sea World. A twelve-thousand-pound killer whale named Tilly attacked a female trainer. The Orca whale grabbed Dawn Brancheau's hair and within minutes she was dead.

The incident generated headlines from coast to coast as experts tried to understand why a killer whale would kill someone. But the headline that intrigued me most came from *The New York Times*.

"Intentions of Whale Killing Are Debated," the article's headline declared. "Questions about the mammal's intent continued to linger."[2]

Well, I'm no expert, but I've seen *Jaws* and *Piranha*. So let me see if I can help out *The New York Times*. Maybe the killer whale whacked the trainer because he was hungry? It's not out of the realm of possibility that even though Sea World refers to them as trainers, the fish refer to them as bait.

Sea World was quick to defend itself in the aftermath of the tragedy. They said they had no reason to suspect the behavior that led to the trainer's death. Well, here's a clue, folks—Tilly is called a "killer" whale.

A number of animal-rights activists were actually siding with the whale, suggesting the creature was overworked and stressed out. But marine conservationist Richard Ellis told *The New York Times* the death of the trainer was not an accident. "This was premeditated," he said.

So how does Sea World punish the whale? Well, that was the subject of great debate.

I had the perfect solution. It involved a rowboat, a shotgun, and Bill Dance.

Cass Sunstein, on the other hand, has a different take on animal rights. He's one of President Obama's pals, and he's a passionate advocate for the furry. He was actually in line for a job in the Obama Administration, but Republican lawmakers objected to Sunstein's desire to establish legal rights for cows and pigs, which would enable animals to file lawsuits in American courts.

No, really.

"There should be extensive regulation of the use of animals in entertainment, scientific experiments, and agriculture,"[3] he wrote in a 2002 working paper while at the University of Chicago Law school.

With all due respect to Mr. Sunstein, I'd like to introduce my own working paper. I like to call it my "Animal Bill of Rights."

1. You have the right to be eaten.
2. You have the right to be batter dipped and skillet fried.
3. You have the right to be smothered in steak sauce.
4. You have the right to be char-grilled.
5. You have the right to be covered in cheese.

It's a dog-eat-dog world out there. And, folks, we have a personal responsibility not to become the main course. Friends, it's time to reclaim our position in the food chain, preferably with a cast-iron skillet in hand. Let the beasts of the field know who's in charge.

May our rally cry be heard across the fruited plain! The only good chicken is a fried chicken.

Just remember, gentle readers, guns don't kill people, but animals do—so be sure to enforce your position on the food chain with your friends from Smith and Wesson.

23

A Conversation with Michelle Malkin

 Michelle Malkin is one of my favorite columnists. She drives liberals nuts with her no-holds-barred approach to writing. But she's also got her finger on the pulse of the mainstream media. And she takes them to task for what she considers to be unfair and unbalanced news coverage. I had a chance to visit with Michelle, and she gave me the inside scoop on what's wrong with American journalism.

Todd: There's no use putting makeup on a pig—so let's get right to it. Is there bias in the mainstream media?

Malkin: There's no question about it. There is bias in the media. There are all sorts of biases. I've worked in daily journalism since 1992 and had the privilege (or ordeal) of working in two metro daily newspaper newsrooms—the *Los Angeles Daily News* and *The Seattle Times*. So when I say, "Yes, there's bias," it's not just the opinion of a conservative pundit who works outside the newsroom but somebody who saw it up close and experienced it personally.

At the *Los Angeles Daily News*, I worked for a center-right-leaning editorial board and didn't spend too much face-to-face contact time with the reporters. But I did have a lot of interaction with beat reporters, and in some cases—this is true with

The Seattle Times as well—it was more the sins of omission than the sins of commission where the bias manifested itself.

I think, in general, there's a generation of newspaper journalists who were inspired by Watergate and had a healthy suspicion of government (which I think is a good thing) but who were very selective in their suspicions. I worked, for example, in cities that were large, major urban cities, dominated by Democratic lawmakers. And when it came to local coverage of city councils or police departments, there tended to be more deference to them, especially when they were doing things that these reporters would obviously have had more questions and complaints about if they were done by Republicans—things like corporate welfare and expanding police authority for the war on drugs.

And then, because public policy issues like race, affirmative action, and similar cultural issues were always (and still are) a big concern and focus of mine, I also saw those biases coming through up there. There's pretty much a knee-jerk support among both the reporters and editorial writers that I worked alongside, support for things like government affirmative action and little questioning of the negative consequences of those kinds of government interventions.

Todd: But when it comes to the Holy Grail of culture war issues—abortion, gay marriage—there seems to be a definite bias.

Malkin: The coverage is almost anthropological. They play Margaret Meade to these alien species of Americans that they have little interaction with, or in common with, on social issues like abortion, gay marriage, immigration.

I definitely saw that in the newsroom. I heard mockery and derision for social conservative activists, particularly activist parents who were trying to fight the spread of left-wing propaganda and curriculum that did not conform with their values and that showed little respect for parental authority.

And that's why, with regards to abortion coverage, what you see is a narrative. A lot of editors will run front-page stories on anti-abortion, pro-life activists who are the most extreme of the movement. And yet there's little coverage when millions of peaceful, normal, everyday, ordinary, pro-life Americans descend on Washington every year for the Pro-Life March.

Little attention is paid to the fact that so many young people are energizing and fusing the movement because, of course, that would destroy their narrative of trying to paint every single pro-life activist as Randall Terry.

Todd: I don't know about you, but I get so frustrated around holidays like Christmas and Easter. We're bombarded with stories that either deride or attempt to debunk the Christian faith.

Malkin: The press simply cannot allow itself to celebrate religious diversity in all of its riches, and yet there almost seems to be this concerted effort every year during religious holidays to tear down the tenets of the Christian faith.

Several years ago I wrote a piece on Easter when I was at *The Seattle Times*, and I criticized our own newsroom because, rather than talk about the religious roots of Easter and what exactly is the reason for the season, it was always this dumbed-down, secularized coverage of Easter, with the Peeps and the Easter eggs.

I quoted an observation Father Richard John Neuhaus made during an interview with a mainstream reporter. The reporter was talking about moral and political corruption and how it was the most unprecedented act of corruption he had seen. Father Neuhaus replied, "Well, we've seen this sort of thing ever since the early days of the Garden."

The reporter just sat there blinking at him and said, "What garden are you speaking about?"

Father's conclusion was that, in some cases, it's not so much simple, ideological, cultural, or political biases. In some cases it's just sheer ignorance.

I think it's a combination of those two things. And certainly I think for Father and Catholic bloggers and Catholics in the media, that ignorance does tend to rear its head in all things related to the pope and the Church and the Vatican.

Todd: Have you ever wondered why the mainstream media has a problem with conservatives?

Malkin: You have to think about the type of people who are motivated to go into journalism and survive journalism school. It tends to be a self-selected and insular clique. That certainly was the case in the newsrooms I worked in.

Fortunately, I was able to work alongside some hardened, old-school journalists who got into the business before it became as professionalized—before you had to have Sorbonne-like documentation to be accepted into the club.

These were the guys who used to store vodka bottles in their drawers back in the day, and they would always grumble to me that it was all those smarty-pants with their MAs that destroyed the profession, and I think there's some truth in that. There wasn't the kind of class diversity there ought to be, especially when these newspapers pride themselves on representing the working class and the everyday people.

Today's journalists live in liberal enclaves. They go to the same cocktail parties and rub elbows with the same people. They're married to the city's power brokers. There's an even more pronounced element of that in newsrooms like *The New York Times*. They have no intellectual curiosity about people who possess opposite or different political views than they do.

Todd: When Anderson Cooper traveled to Nashville, Tennessee, in 2010 to cover the historic floods, he seemed like he was on a different planet. He marveled at the number of churches and the fact that people were actually helping their neighbors. He seemed genuinely shocked and amazed.

Malkin: Anderson Cooper a Vanderbilt. You look at people like that, who have traveled around the world, and yet they treat their own fellow Americans like, again, alien species. *The New York Times* has that same approach as the CNN journalists, of parachuting into these little corners of America and just being completely amazed and dazzled by the exoticness of it.

Todd: In 2008, President Obama used the phrase "bitter Americans that cling to their guns and religion." From a media standpoint, do you think journalists "get" middle America? Do you think they get those so-called "bitter Americans"?

Malkin: They haven't for a long time. That phrase, I think, encapsulates how many of Obama's water carriers in the media feel about the people they cover and the people they feel are entitled to buy their newspapers.

Just look at the allergic reaction of the media to the Tea Party Movement. The taxpayer revolts of 2010 were really revelatory. The viciousness and vindictiveness with which journalists treated this national movement was incredible.

Todd: So how about Michelle Malkin? Are you one of President Obama's "bitter Americans"?

Malkin: That was one of the biggest myths of how the press portrayed the Tea Party Movement, and it is certainly a persistent myth about conservatives who fight for limited government.

In fact, I start every day blessed, with a smile on my face, counting myself among the luckiest people on the planet, to be able to live in this country, exercise free speech and freedom of assembly, and to be able to petition—still—for redress of grievances.

You want to talk about bitter and clingy? Look at the teachers union. Look at the Service Employees International Union. They were the ones who sent their thugs out to peaceful protests of Tea Party activists.

Look at where the real rancor was during the town hall protests over the summer of Obamacare. It was the Organizing for America and Media Matters types who were the most bitter and angry.

Most of the conservatives I cover are happy warriors, in the mold of Ronald Reagan. Are we upset? Are we worried? Are we concerned about our kids' future? Yes.

But ultimately, there are things outside the Beltway, outside the political square, that buoy us. And those include the things a lot of these left-wing reporters do not appreciate or understand—community, school life, and church.

Todd: What are the dangers of a press that is not fair and balanced?

Malkin: The founders enshrined a free press for a reason, as an independent check on the power of government. And when the mainstream press fills that role, it's wonderful.

I'm not a blanket detractor of every single journalist in the mainstream media. I've worked in the mainstream media. I'm a part of it. I owe so much of my early career and my ability to jump into the Internet to the great editors and veteran journalists I've learned so much from. The danger is in becoming so intertwined with the people you're covering that you're unable to do your job.

I think we saw that in living color, in such *vibrant* color, during the 2008 presidential campaign. When the Grand Canyon-sized gap between Barack Obama's rhetoric and the reality of his Chicago politics was so obvious to a lot of people, and yet was not covered by the press—in fact was covered up—I think the press lost so much credibility, they became a joke. You had these reporters who were gushing over Obama's physique—you remember that? There was that *Washington Post* reporter who talked about the sun-kissed glint off his chest?

It's a huge squandering of those inalienable rights that were passed on to us, not to forsake the basic duties of the press, which is, to borrow that 1970s phrase, *question authority*. We need watchdogs, not lapdogs.

24

The Rise of the Food Nazis

The government is coming after your Nutter Butters. There's a national movement underway to control what we eat. I call these people Food Nazis, lawmakers who are legislating our taste buds. They want to come into our homes, clean out our refrigerators, and force us to eat meals only the government deems appropriate.

First Lady Michelle Obama has been at the forefront of this effort, the country's self-anointed First Parent. Her work started at the White House with the planting of a special garden. You might remember seeing photographs of Mrs. Obama tending her garden in a pair of $495 Tory Burch gardening boots—because that's how regular Americans tend *their* gardens.

Then there was the time she scolded the nation's restaurants. She delivered an address to the National Restaurant Association and told them to take butter and cream out of their dishes and use low-fat milk and provide carrots on kids' menus. She even suggested they make French fries a "special order" item.

She also championed a child nutrition bill that gave the government power to limit school bake sales and other fund-raisers. Her "Let's Move" campaign has generated outrage among millions of Americans.

Perhaps we should be reminded of the words of Thomas

Jefferson. "A government big enough to give you everything you want is strong enough to take everything you have," he said.

Sean Hannity summed up the issue on FOX News Channel. He said the First Lady was "taking the nanny state to a new level by telling us what to eat."

"Get away from my french fries, Mrs. Obama," declared Glenn Beck.

Sarah Palin also chimed in by preparing a plate of s'mores on her television show, *Sarah Palin's Alaska*. "This is in honor of Michelle Obama, who said the other day we should not have dessert," she said. She expounded on her comments during a radio interview with Laura Ingraham.

"What she is telling us is she cannot trust parents to make decisions for their own children, for their own families in what we should eat," Palin said. "Instead of a government thinking that they need to take over and make decisions for us according to some politician or politician's wife's priorities, just leave us alone, get off our back, and allow us as individuals to exercise our own God-given rights to make our own decisions, and then our country gets back on the right track."

The mainstream media went nuts over Palin's statement, but she has a point. We have a God-given right in this nation to eat whatever we want to, whether it's tofu or deep-fried butter. And we also have the right to suffer the consequences of our actions.

Perhaps Mrs. Obama might want to clean out her own refrigerator before cleaning out ours. Consider the menu for the 2011 White House Super Bowl Party:

- Bratwurst
- Kielbasa
- Cheeseburgers
- Deep-dish pizza
- Buffalo wings
- German potato salad
- Twice-baked potatoes
- Potato chips and pretzels

- Chips and dips
- Ice cream

I'm hard-pressed to find a single piece of arugula on that menu.

This nanny-state mentality was put on display for the entire country to watch during a live episode of the ABC talk show *The View*. If you haven't seen the program, it features Barbara Walters and a bunch of liberal women ranting and raving about various issues of the day. I personally don't watch *The View* because I can't handle that much testosterone in the morning.

But one day Paula Deen was invited on the program to talk about a new cookbook for children. Everything good about the South is wrapped up in Paula Deen. She is kind and compassionate, slow to anger, and knows that the way to a man's heart is slathered in butter.

Miss Paula arrived on the show with a basketful of homemade treats, as any southern lady worth her drawl would do. While the other hosts were nibbling away, Paula noticed Barbara Walters was not eating.

"Barbara, you're not diving in," she said.

And that's when Barbara tore into the queen of southern cooking on national television.

"Let me act like your mother and ask you to hold off a minute," Barbara sneered. "This is a cookbook for kids. Obesity is the number-one problem for kids today. Everything you have here is enormously fattening. You tell kids to have cheesecake for breakfast. You tell them to have chocolate cake and meatloaf for lunch. And french fries. Doesn't it even bother you that you're adding to this?"

So it's Paula Deen's fault that the nation's children are overweight? Give me a break. Miss Paula was gracious in her response to the ranting of a lunatic who was apparently delusional from eating too much granola.

"I think we have to teach our children, first off, Barbara, moderation," she replied.

Barbara fired back, "Not when you're giving them this."

Now, if Miss Paula had been a redneck woman, she would have politely removed her high heels, taken off her earrings, and promptly commenced to giving Barbara Walters the catfight she deserved. Fortunately for Barbara, Miss Paula is a refined and cultured southern lady.

I had a chance to ask Miss Paula about that during a special meeting in New York City. She was in town to help distribute free Smithfield hams to families in need. Southern folks do that kind of thing.

Todd: My Aunt Lynn from Coldwater, Mississippi, said you should've grabbed a cast-iron skillet and whacked Barbara Walters on the head.

Miss Paula: It sounded like Barbara wanted to blame me for childhood obesity. I don't have any obese children in my family. So I don't know where that was coming from. I encourage children and families to eat nutritiously and to eat in moderation. But the biggest thing is they need to get off the sofa and get outside and play and exercise.

Todd: So you don't eat deep-fried butter every day?

Miss Paula: I don't. You know, people think, "Gosh, she eats fried chicken and biscuits and gravy every day of her life." I do not. But when I do eat fried chicken, it's prepared the old southern way, the way that my granny taught me how to cook it.

Todd: What is it about food?

Miss Paula: Food is the vehicle that takes us where we want to go. It's the common denominator between all of us. It doesn't matter what your race is, your religion, where you live. We all have to eat to survive.

Todd: And there's nothing better than southern cooking.

Miss Paula: Ain't nothing better than southern cooking, baby.

And then Miss Paula gave me a bear hug. I'm ready to go to heaven now.

Cheese, Oreos Banned from School

American cheese and Oreo cookies are banned from packed lunches at the Children's Success Academy in Tucson, Arizona. The school has a strict policy forbidding any processed foods, refined sugar, or even white flour. At the start of every school day, boys and girls at the public charter school are required to allow teachers to inspect their lunch boxes. Any forbidden foods are confiscated, and students are given a "healthy alternative."

"I will get them peanut butter and honey on whole wheat,"[1] teacher Leticia Moreno told the *Arizona Daily Star*. However, the peanut butter can't have any sugar.

The school doesn't have a cafeteria so students must bring their own lunch; and according to the newspaper, the rules are creating a hardship for cash-strapped parents.

"It is challenging mainly because in grocery stores it's so hard to find anything without sugar," parent Breanna Chacon told the newspaper.

The list of banned foods is substantial—American cheese, canned fruit, flavored yogurt, white bread, peanut butter made with sugar, and even Oreo cookies. One child had a package of Ritz crackers and cheese spread confiscated by the Food Nazis.

And there are no exceptions to the rule, said Nanci Aiken, the school's director. "You don't need a cake," she said. "They can have nuts or fruit."

Speaking of nuts . . .

"I feel like the Wicked Witch of the West a lot of times, but it makes such a big difference," she said. "When you eat sugar, especially by itself like a candy bar, you get a rush and crash. An apple will not give you instant gratification or a rush, but it lasts longer."

There are critics to the school's methods. "All kinds of emotional and behavioral problems can happen if you tell a child never, ever to eat a cookie," said registered dietitian Nancy Rogers. "They may do just the opposite once they are at a rebellious stage."

But, said Aiken, "We are what we eat."

They're facing a similar issue in the British town of Pemberton. Dorothy Gallear removed her son from a nursery after the family was rebuked for serving the child a cheese sandwich. She was told that future cheese sandwiches must include either lettuce or tomato. Otherwise, the sandwich would be classified as a snack and therefore would be banned under government guidelines.

"I think it's absolutely pathetic, and these people are playing Big Brother with people's lives," said Mrs. Gallear in an interview with *The Telegraph*. "They were looking down their noses at me."[2]

The family put the boy in a new school where he was allowed to eat cheese.

University Bans Meat

Imagine walking into the dining hall at Bowdoin College after a long day of mindless lectures—your mind set on a thick, juicy cheeseburger. But instead of grilled meat, the lunch ladies plop a steaming pile of stir-fry tofu on your plate.

Welcome to the reality for meat lovers at Maine's Bowdoin College. The university endorsed a mandatory program called "Meatless Monday" in the school's dining halls. No burgers, no fried chicken, not even Vienna sausages. Instead students were served vegetables and tofu.

You can blame the antimeat campaign on the school's progressive College Democrats. They said it was a way to promote healthy eating. The Democrats-in-training also believe eating fewer animals will help the environment, presumably by cutting down on the amount of methane gas released into the atmosphere. I take it they've never been around anyone who's eaten a pound of steamed broccoli.

Fortunately, meat-eaters at Bowdoin College refused to bow to the liberal philosophy of "do as I say, whether you like it or not."

"Raising awareness for a cause is one thing, but to have a vocal minority impose its will onto the rest of us and then attempt to stifle dissent is outrageous,"[3] wrote Sam Landis in an e-mail to *The Bowdoin Orient* newspaper.

Landis and another student organized a counterprotest. They gave away free McDonalds double cheeseburgers to anyone who agreed to donate to the Coastal Humane Society. Other students protested by hauling around buckets of KFC and offering chicken legs to grateful classmates. At least one group bought some charcoal and fired up a barbecue.

So how did the progressive and tolerant liberals respond? They tore down the posters promoting the event.

The college said the "Meatless Monday" was well received by students but acknowledged a drop in the number of diners. They predicted other meatless days in the future.

So if the students boycotted the dining hall on Meatless Monday, where did they eat dinner? A reporter for *The Bowdoin Orient* tracked down most of the student body at Jack Magee's Pub. The restaurant was offering a special Monday night meal— bacon cheeseburgers.

Kathryn Shaw, one of the organizers of Meatless Monday, said she was dismayed that many students ate meat. "It frustrated me that students weren't willing to try it,"[4] she told *Inside Higher Ed*. "Because you missed the table—whether you were supportive or not—and missed the opportunity to try the protein-filled vegetarian options that were offered, and we missed out on a conversation. It was certainly their choice though."

It certainly was, Miss Shaw. And they chose to eat a protein-filled cow instead.

Young Lady, Step Away from the Jolly Rancher

Leighann Adair was in big trouble. The third-grader at Brazos Elementary School in Texas was caught red-handed with contraband in the cafeteria. She was promptly dispatched to the principal's office where she was given a week's detention. So what was the little girl's crime? She was caught with a Jolly Rancher.

It wasn't even a full bag of Jolly Ranchers. But in Orchard, Texas, possession of a single Jolly Rancher candy is a punishable crime. The Brazos County school superintendent defended the harsh sentence, saying he was complying with a state law that limits junk food in schools and bans "minimal nutrition" foods. "Whether or not I agree with the guidelines, we have to follow the rules,"[5] Superintendent Jack Ellis told KHOU-TV.

Leighann's mom said it's a huge overreaction. "I think it's stupid to give a kid a week's worth of detention for a piece of candy," said Amber Brazda. "The whole thing was just ridiculous to me."

But the superintendent said the ten-year-old needed to be taught a lesson. He also said the school's federal funding could have been jeopardized by the Jolly Rancher.

Federal funding was also jeopardized at the Fairmount Elementary School in Pennsylvania. That's why the lunch ladies only gave students a single chicken finger for lunch, along with a two-ounce scoop of macaroni and cheese. But don't blame the lunch ladies; blame the government.

"These kids were absolutely crying that they were starving when they got out of school,"[6] parent Marlene George told the *Valley News Dispatch*. Holly Pukal's daughter also attends the elementary school. Her child was so hungry she took her to Subway to get something to eat.

"She came out of school, and she was just starved," she told the newspaper.

Sharon Conway, director of food service for the Highlands School District, confirmed the less-than-bountiful lunch menu. She said it was partially her fault for serving both macaroni-and-cheese and chicken on the same menu. "When you looked at it, it just did not look like much," she told the local newspaper. "Yet they were getting what they were supposed to get."

According to state guidelines, children are only allowed to receive two ounces of protein in their lunches. The mac-and-cheese represented one ounce, leaving room for only one chicken tender. She said the cafeteria must follow state guidelines; otherwise their funding could be jeopardized.

Is anyone ready to homeschool?

Cupcakes Outlawed

The Food Nazis in South Redford, Michigan, have banned birthday cupcakes at Vandenberg Elementary School. God forbid boys and girls are treated to a tasty celebratory snack. Principal Syndee Malek said she wanted her students to eat healthier food, and that meant putting an end to the longtime classroom tradition.

"I know we're not the first school to do it,"[7] Malek told WDIV-TV, arguing she doesn't want to take up classroom time with unhealthy foods.

Lady, it's a cupcake.

But the Goodie Gestapo didn't stop at cupcakes. School clubs are not allowed to sell junk food. Even pizza parties have been banned. So instead of an occasional slice of cheese and pepperoni, the kids are rewarded by taking daily walks. No wonder so many folks are homeschooling.

But it gets worse, folks. The lunchroom at Vandenberg has undergone an extreme makeover. Fried foods have been banned. They've been replaced with fresh fruit and vegetables.

School leaders said they still allow the kids to eat hot dogs. But there's a catch. The hotdogs are made with turkey.

"This is why I pay for a private school," one parent wrote to the local newspaper. "The kids get a great education that gets them ready for college. They can eat cupcakes and burn off the calories at recess and gym class."

It sounds like the moms and dads of South Redford are pretty reasonable folks. It's too bad none of them work for the school system.

Home-Cooking Banned!

The Little Village Academy personifies the Food Nazi movement. The all-knowing principal banned lunches from home. Principal Elsa Carmona didn't mince words, arguing that the lunch ladies prepared better meals than moms do.

"Nutrition-wise, it is better for the children to eat at the school," she told the *Chicago Tribune*. "It's about the nutrition and the excellent-quality food they are able to serve. It's milk versus a Coke."[8] That's the first time I've ever heard the words "excellent" and "quality" used to describe mystery meat.

Principal Carmona explained that banning lunches from home was the only way to crack down on kids bringing junk food to school. But the real issue here is control. The school is saying they know better than the parents.

And now there's a full-scale revolt at the school.

"We should bring our own lunch! We should bring our own lunch! We should bring our own lunch!" students chanted when a reporter from the paper visited the cafeteria one day, according to AOL News.[9]

Amie Hamlin is the executive director of the New York Coalition for Healthy School Food. She said banning homemade lunches was a bit of a stretch, but she understood why the principal was overruling parents.

"I see the junk that kids bring in," Hamlin told AOL News. "But some parents want their kids to eat only organic or vegan, and those parents should not be undermined. Sometimes meals from home are much healthier." Well, what about the rights of parents who want their kids to eat peanut butter and jelly or ham and cheese? Aren't they being undermined?

My mother used to pack some pretty tasty lunches when I was in grade school. My favorite was her country-fried steak sandwich, a staple of southern cooking. I can only imagine what would have happened if a teacher had confiscated my sandwich and gave me a celery stalk with a cup of soy milk. I suspect it would have involved a cast-iron skillet though.

To Principal Carmona, I say keep your hands out of other people's lunch boxes. And to the people of Chicago, I say keep the faith. United we stand; divided we eat tofu.

New York City Wants to Ban Salt

New York City is the birthplace of the Food Nazis. They've already banned blueberry muffins and brownies in public schools. Then they banned trans fat and ordered restaurants to post calorie counts on their menus. Now the Big Apple has declared a war against salt.

Mayor Michael Bloomberg is pushing a plan to cut the amount of salt in restaurant food and packaged food by 25 percent. He's our Democrat-turned-Republican-turned-Independent mayor. Bloomberg believes salt is just as bad as asbestos.

"If we know there's asbestos in a schoolroom, what do you expect us to do?" Bloomberg asked. "Say it's not our business? I don't think so. The same thing is true with food and smoking and a lot of things.

"Salt and asbestos, clearly both are bad for you," he said. "Modern medicine thinks you shouldn't be smoking if you want to live longer. Modern medicine thinks you shouldn't be eating salt, or sodium."

Well, you shouldn't be eating shards of glass either. Does that mean we should ban windows?

The salt reduction is not going over well with many chefs. The owner of the Momofuku Noodle Bar called it "stupid and foolish."

"I'm all for trying to make New Yorkers healthier people, but when it comes to him telling me how much salt to put in food, I have a problem with it,"[10] said Ed Brown in an interview with the *New York Post*. He owns a restaurant on the city's Upper West Side.

But if Assemblyman Felix Ortiz has his way, the entire state could be subjected to a ban on salt. He's introduced legislation to criminalize the use of salt in restaurants.

"No owner or operator of a restaurant in this state shall use salt in any form in the preparation of any food for consumption by customers of such restaurant, including food prepared to be consumed on the premises of such restaurant or off of such premises," his legislation states. Anyone caught violating the ban would face a $1,000 fine for each violation. Did you ever imagine a time in this nation's history when chefs would be hauled to jail in handcuffs for sprinkling salt on french fries?

That's not all. The Education Department implemented a ban on bake sales. The new wellness policy also placed limits on what schools can sell in vending machines and student-run stores. "I think it's kind of pointless," Eli Salamon-Abrams told *The New York Times*. "I mean, why can't we have bake sales?"[11]

Students used the bake sales to raise money for field trips, uniforms, and equipment. Education officials suggested kids could still raise money by hosting walkathons or selling key chains. Let's be honest, folks. Given the choice, would a teenager fork over cash for a double fudge brownie or a carrot stick?

They're even going after Ronald McDonald and Colonel Sanders. Lawmakers on both coasts are trying to ban fast food restaurants. New York City Councilman Eric Gioa said he wants to prohibit restaurants from operating stores near public schools.

"Banning fast food around schools will have a measurable impact on student's lives,"[12] he told *The Epoch Times*. Some national advocacy groups actually believe restaurants like McDonalds and Burger King are predators, and children are the victims. "NAAO believes predatory marketing of junk food escalates the child obesity health crisis," Meme Roth, president of National Action Against Obesity told *The Epoch Times*.

In San Francisco they're trying to outlaw Happy Meal toys. Apparently city leaders believe dictating what kind of plastic toys McDonalds can give away will lead to slimmer children.

They literally believe the government has a responsibility to step in and make sure young boys and girls are eating healthy food. I believe San Francisco resident Deborah Jackson speaks for all of us burger-loving bitter Americans. "Look, my daughter is eating her lunch, she likes it, she likes the toy," she told the *San Francisco Chronicle*, while eating at McDonalds. "We don't eat here every day, not even once a week, but when we do come, it's a treat, and I don't want that messed with."[13]

Dispatches from the Schoolhouse

25

Jumping Off the GW Bridge—Sorry

 I never met Tyler Clementi, but I was profoundly moved by his story. He was a son. He was a brother.

He was, by all accounts, a gentle soul—a lover of music, a gifted violinist whose work was called distinguished. And the eighteen-year-old freshman at Rutgers University was also the keeper of a secret.

Robert Righthand knew about the secret. He was Tyler's friend. They grew up together in Ridgewood, New Jersey.

"I can tell you that whatever state he was in, he had it in reserve for a very long time,"[1] Righthand told the *New York Post*.

"You never thought he was depressed," he said. "You just thought he was quiet."

Dharun Ravi also new about Tyler's secret, and on September 19, he decided to do the unthinkable—he shared Tyler's secret with the world.

In the privacy of his dorm room, the young violinist engaged in a romantic encounter. And in no way am I condoning his behavior. But Tyler had no idea his roommate was also engaged in something—the ultimate betrayal. Every move, every intimate moment was being secretly recorded and streamed live on the Internet.

Ravi, and fellow freshman Molly Wei, remotely accessed the feed and saw Tyler and his friend.

"Roommate asked for the room till midnight," Ravi tweeted to his friends. In a matter of moments, Tyler's private life became public. "I went into Molly's room and turned on my Webcam. I saw him making out with a dude. Yay."

It's unclear how many people actually saw the video. But the damage had been done. Word began to spread, and students began to gossip. For Tyler it was the beginning of the end.

Tyler's parents were not aware of his secret until they heard a knock at the front door.

A police officer explained to the couple that their son had parked his car on the New Jersey side of the Hudson River. They said he posted a final message on his Facebook page and then began the long walk over the George Washington Bridge.

"Jumping off the GW Bridge. Sorry."

And so it happened that the soft-spoken boy with sandy hair stopped and climbed over the railing. A witness said the anguished young man paused for a moment, and then Tyler Clementi plunged into eternity.

Dharun Ravi and Molly Wei will answer for their alleged crimes, but the damage that's been caused is irreversible.

In this age of social networking, privacy is becoming an ancient relic. Lives can be changed by the posting of a single photo or profile update. And in the case of Tyler, lives can be lost in 140 characters or less.

What kind of people find joy and comfort in the misfortunes of others? What kind of people find pleasure in exploiting the secret places of another's life? Again, I'm not siding with this young man's actions. But have we reached an age in this nation where destroying lives has become something of a spectator sport?

The days following Tyler's suicide were filled with pundits pontificating, politicians politicking, and advocates advocating— all trying to twist and turn the private hurts of Tyler into whatever fit their agenda.

But far away from the ranting and the rhetoric, a New Jersey family endures heartbreak. We know that time passes and seasons fade, but for the Clementi family, time stands still. They mourn for a son who will never come home, a life that will never be lived. The melodies and harmonies that once filled their Ridgewood, New Jersey, home are gone—replaced with a haunting silence.

And as I write these words, I can't help but wonder, how many more Tylers are out there, waiting for someone to push them over the edge.

Homecoming Queens, Kings, and Jokers

The new homecoming queen at The College of William and Mary is a mary. Students have elected a transgender homecoming queen. Jessee Vasold was crowned during halftime of the Virginia school's football game against James Madison. Vasold prefers to be called a "genderqueer."

For those of you who grew up when God only created men and women, *genderqueer* means William and Mary's homecoming queen has all the commensurate body parts of a king. Genderqueer people apparently don't adhere to either strictly male or strictly female gender roles.

Yet the nation's second-oldest college is overwhelmingly supportive of their new queen.

"I've only had people congratulating me. I know that one of my friends was in a conversation with someone who didn't think it was fair that I was able to run because I'm not female-bodied," Vasold told *The Flat Hat*, the college's student newspaper. "But it generated a really good conversation, so they were able to talk about a lot of different things."[1]

University officials are just tickled pink to have a genderqueer homecoming queen. "William and Mary is a diverse and inclusive community, and student selections to this year's homecoming court reflect that,"[2] school spokesman Brian Whitson told local news-papers in an e-mail. If that's the case, William and Mary must be home to an unusually large number of genderqueer students.

Whoever said homecoming dances are a drag?

Gender-benders are not just limited to colleges. And that brings us to Fairfax High School in Southern California. Last year Sergio Garcia (not the professional golfer) became one of the first males on the west coast to be elected prom queen. To his credit, Garcia chose to wear a suit instead of pantyhose. "But don't be fooled, deep down inside, I am a queen,"[3] the eighteen-year-old told the *Los Angeles Times*.

Among his detractors were a number of high school girls who wondered why he didn't run for prom king. But supporters said Garcia's election was a significant step in breaking homosexual stereotypes. Following his reign, he hopes to pursue his dream of becoming a choreographer and hairdresser.

And then there's the story of what happened at George Mason University. Students elected Ryan Allen as their homecoming queen. Allen is gay. The twenty-two-year-old junior is also a drag queen and goes by the name Reann Ballslee.

Allen was crowned during halftime of the men's basketball game. He accepted his tiara wearing a sequined top and size twelve pumps.

Two other contestants actually had functioning female parts, but Allen was able to garner the most votes. He won a qualifying pageant for the contest by performing a Britney Spears song wearing a silver bra and zebra-print pants.

You might be surprised to learn that not everyone at George Mason is happy with their homecoming queen. Some even said their "miss" who is a "mister" was an embarrassment.

But don't count George Mason's administration among the offended. The university spokesman told *The Washington Post* they were "very comfortable" with the choice.[4] The school, he said, does not require participants in the Mr. and Ms. Mason pageant to compete along precise gender lines.

Vickie Kirsch, the director of George Mason's Women and Gender Studies Department, was overjoyed. She told reporters the choice was "a significant and positive benchmark in Mason's history."

So in that alternate universe known as academia, a homosexual wearing female panties is one small step for man, one giant benchmark for George Mason University.

The student newspaper, the *Broadside*, hailed the newly crowned queen. Allen was given a "thumbs up" for "being an outstanding representative of Mason."[5]

And why wouldn't they be proud of a young man wearing zebra-print pants, lip-synching to a Britney Spears song? It's the pinnacle of diversity and inclusiveness.

Meanwhile, I've been wondering about the homecoming dance between Mr. and Ms. Mason.

Who led?

27

Rub a Dub Dub

Editor's note: The following chapter contains some instances of graphic language necessary to communicate the severity of the subject matter. So you might want to set down your iced tea.

 Jack and Jill went up the hill and did something incredibly inappropriate, according to a comprehensive sex education plan in Helena, Montana, that would begin teaching the subject to students as early as kindergarten age. The Helena Public School System plan proposes introducing first graders to the idea that people can be attracted to the same gender. In second grade, students are instructed to avoid gay slurs. And by the time students turn ten years old, they are taught about various types of intercourse. By grade five, the subject matter becomes even more vivid and descriptive. Shocking. If I don't want to talk about it *here*, makes you wonder why it seems appropriate *there*.

Jeff Laszloffy, of the Montana Family Foundation, is among those outraged that educators want to teach sex education to kindergartners. "It's absolutely insane," Laszloffy said. "This is not education. This has crossed the line and has gone from education to indoctrination, and that's the problem parents have.

"This is not the reason we send our kids to school—to be indoctrinated on different sex positions," he said. "These types of conversations should be had between parents and their children at the appropriate time, and we don't think it's the state's job to determine when that time is."

School Superintendent Bruce Messinger told me parents have fair questions about the content of the plan. "This is by design a formative process," he said, noting the section about human sexuality has drawn the most attention.

He said educators are still looking at the age appropriateness of the material and said final decisions won't be made until August. "There will be plenty of time for public comment," he said. "We are working through how the content would be taught and how the curriculum would be presented to students."

He said the school system stresses parental involvement and said anyone with objections to classroom material has the option of pulling their child out of the class.

"We honor that," he said.

But he defends teaching sex education in grade school based on national data that he said indicates a growing number of ten-, eleven-, and twelve-year-olds becoming sexually active.

Laszloffy counters by saying that the bottom line is this: the program puts government between parents and their children. "It tramples parental rights, and we think those rights need to be upheld," he said.

The debate over whether to teach and what to teach kindergartners has been raging for years. In 2007 then Senator Barack Obama said he supported sex education for kindergartners—calling it "the right thing to do." Obama recounted how grade school sex education became a campaign issue during his 2004 senate race against Alan Keyes.

"I remember him using this in his campaign against me," Obama told Planned Parenthood as he mimicked Keyes, "Barack Obama supports teaching sex education to kindergartners, which—I didn't know what to tell him, but it's the right thing to do—to provide age-appropriate sex education, science-based sex education in schools."

A wide number of parents who live in Montana, though, are adamantly opposed to the plan that's being considered in their state. Many say it's not the school's responsibility to teach such graphic material to their children. Others call it a disgrace.

"Outrage," said Shannon Karp of Belgrade. "We are just setting children up to start having sex at an earlier age. I think we should let our children be children. Let them be innocent and enjoy their grade school years. There will be enough pressure on them as they get older."

Well said.

Meanwhile, school leaders in Provincetown, Massachusetts, approved a measure that will provide free condoms to elementary school students. The policy, unanimously approved by the Provincetown School Committee, does not include an age limit, meaning children of any age can ask for and receive free condoms.

The committee also directed school leaders not to honor requests from any parent who might object to their child's receiving condoms. In other words, you don't have a right, mommy and daddy, to prevent your seven-year-old from getting a contraceptive device if he or she wants one.

The policy does stipulate, however, that kids must consult with a nurse or trained counselor before getting their sexual protection—a provision that surprisingly upset some of the committee members,[1] according to the *Provincetown Banner*.

"I can see some kids opting out because of the conversation. I'm not against [the policy]. I'm just trying to put myself in that teenager's spot," said committee member Carrie Notaro.

"I don't like that students can't be discreet about this," committee member Shannon Patrick told the newspaper. "They have to go and ask for it. I'd rather them not have the conservation [with counselors] and have the condom than not have the condom."

School Superintendent Beth Singer, on the other hand, supported the instructional aspect of the rule, explaining that younger boys and girls might not be experienced in such adult matters. "We're talking about younger kids," she told the newspaper. "They have questions they need answered on how to use them, when to use them."

Reaction has been mixed on newspaper Web sites. One reader opposed to the measure wrote, "A condom distribution policy at the elementary school? Twelve-year-old kids need condoms? When I was twelve, I thought a peck on the lips was something."

Another reader wrote, "Stupidity exists everywhere. Why not just give the kids free needles while we're at it?"

However, a supporter of the measure praised committee members. "If the kids really are sexually active that young these days, then they absolutely should have access to condoms. Sure, it's demoralizing to think of eleven- and twelve-year-olds starting at that age, but if they are, they're not going to stop."

This must be the sentiment in Philadelphia, as well, where children as young as eleven years old are not only allowed but are encouraged to get free condoms. The condoms are paid for by taxpayers, and according to the health department's Web site, "If you live in Philadelphia and you are between the ages of eleven and nineteen, all you have to do is fill out the form below, and we'll put together a package for you."

Ronnie Polaneczky, a columnist for the *Philadelphia Daily News*, exposed the health department's perverse desire to equip young boys and girls with sex tools without their parent's knowledge or consent.[2] This is happening within a context where, according to the executive director of one local nonprofit that works to prevent the spread of HIV, "Teachers call us because their kids are acting out sexually. They'll catch them in the bathroom or the stairwell. They hear that kids are cutting school to have orgies." Philadelphia's health commissioner told the newspaper that approximately 25 percent of the eleven-year-olds in West Philadelphia are sexually active. *Eleven-year-olds!*

I'm not a professional educator, of course, but maybe if the school system would stop teaching third-graders how to have sex, they wouldn't have so big a problem.

The sexual indoctrination of boys and girls isn't limited to the West or Northeast, however. Parents in Shenandoah, Iowa, were outraged after fourteen-year-olds were instructed on graphic sexual acts during a Planned Parenthood sex education class at the local high school.

"It was horribly inappropriate," Colleen Dostal told me. "To do that in a mixed-gender classroom, I truly believe it was inappropriate."

Dostal's fourteen-year-old son was one of a handful of eighth-graders in the class. The students, she said, were given instruction on how to perform female exams, and the instructor used a 3D, anatomically correct male sex organ to explain how to use a condom.

But Dostal said she was most upset over the instructor simulating sexual acts using stuffed animals designed to resemble STDs. "I do not understand why any adult with a classroom of children would show them sexual positions," she said. "I think that's horribly inappropriate."

"Had we known this was going on, I would have sat in the classroom, or I would have pulled him out," Dostal said.

She took her concerns to the principal, whom Dostal said was "mortified" and willingly apologized. Still, several other parents decided to take the issue to the school superintendent, including one parent who said, "I understand it's a state law that sex education be taught, but it is also state mandated that parents be told that this is going to happen, and we were not told."

Planned Parenthood's Jennifer Horner, for her part, defended the class and said some of the material had been misconstrued. "We are not trying to keep any of this a secret," she told the newspaper. "All information we use is medically accurate and science-based."

Superintendent Dick Profit told the *Omaha World-Herald* he actually received an equal number of calls both supporting and opposing the Planned Parenthood presentation. "It's a political hot potato; it's a religious hot potato; it's a parental hot potato,"[3] he told the newspaper. "It's all of these things that cause a crack in the system between society, parents, and schools, and we're still required to do it."

He said parents and guardians will receive advance warning next year about the class. But that may not satisfy parents like Scott Gray, whose sixteen-year-old son was in the class. "As far as we were concerned, it wasn't sex ed.; it was sex demonstration," he told the newspaper.

I could go on.

I could tell about the sex lessons described in books that, according to the Christian Institute, a British advocacy group, are meant to be read by five-year-olds.

I could tell about the provocative survey sent out to seventh-graders at Hardy Middle School in Washington, DC, asking about the students' sexual orientations, the date of their last HIV test, and the precise extent of their sexual experience.

I could tell about the eight-hour leadership class attended by Hillsboro High School seniors in Nashville, Tennessee, that at one point (for some reason) included a demonstration from representatives of a local AIDS education organization, complete with anatomical models that left little if anything to the imagination.

I could tell about a lot of things.

But let me just say this for the sake of full disclosure: I don't have children. I'm simply a taxpayer who foots the bill for their free condoms, sex education classes, Planned Parenthood abortions, and STD medications. And I'm really not sure why all these government leaders and education leaders are sweating the growing number of kids engaging in sexual activity. Instead of being shocked, they should be celebrating. These esteemed educators have taken sexually charged, hormone-crazed teenagers and given them the tools to use what the good Lord gave them. And judging from the nation's teenage pregnancy rates, I'd say they've done a pretty good job.

But if school leaders are truly wanting to curb teen sex—if that's the case—I've got the perfect solution for them: stop teaching how-to classes and start teaching don't-do classes.

I know the experts are throwing out all sorts of statistics these days, but there's only one statistic they need to arm themselves with. Exactly 100 percent of American teenagers who practice abstinence do not become pregnant. Until the schools start living with that, why not stick to the reading and writing and leave the child-rearing to the experts?

And a word of advice to moms and dads: try acting like your child's parent instead of their friend. Stop letting your daughters walk out of the house dressed like high-priced hookers. Start telling your sons how to treat ladies—with respect and dignity.

In the meantime, though, if your first-grader comes home and says he read *Rub-a-Dub-Dub, Three Men in a Tub*, don't assume it's a nursery rhyme.

28

Tag—You're Out

 It was bound to happen sooner or later—recess has been outlawed. And you can blame the demise of fun-time on the most violent schoolyard game ever concocted—*dodgeball*.

Jump rope? Don't even think about it.

Hopscotch? Kid, you're just asking for trouble.

Tag? Don't make me taser you, bro.

The assault on recess started in earnest at the turn of the century. Franklin Elementary School in Santa Monica, California, for example, decided to ban the game of tag because it created self-esteem issues among the less athletically inclined boys and girls.

Principal Pat Samarge told parents children were suffering physical and emotional injuries. "Little kids were coming in and saying, 'I don't like it.' [The] children weren't feeling good about it,"[1] he said in a 2002 FOX News report.

Heaven forbid children learn that winning and losing is a part of life. And that's the point Tamara Silver tried to make to the school. "I want my child to know that he can have some freedom," she told FOX. "I want my child to know he can play. I want my child to know that he call fall down and skin his knee."

But Ms. Silver's opinion is not shared by those uber-intelligent folks who run the nation's school systems. Places like

Cheyenne, Wyoming, and Charleston, South Carolina, and Spokane, Washington, have banned playground activities such as soccer and touch football.

USA Today reported on educators who worried about "kids running into one another" and getting hurt.[2] That's why the appropriately named Freedom Elementary School in Cheyenne, Wyoming, decided to tag out tag.

The Oakdale School in Montville, Connecticut, decided to cut out traditional recess altogether. *The New York Times* reported in 2007 on their progressive approach to educating children.[3] Kids were banned from vigorous games of tag and other "body-banging" activities because school leaders were afraid feelings might get bruised.

Parents made such a fuss that the school decided to modify their rules—allowing kids to play kickball—but only if no one kept score.

Here's what irate mommy Shari Clewell told *The New York Times*: "Life is competitive. Kids compete for attention. They compete for grades. You compete for a job. You compete from the time you're little all the way to the end."

Oh, Shari! Sweet, naïve Shari. If only you had been educated in child-rearing by childless, intellectual elites!

My favorite story comes from Broadway Elementary School in Newark, New Jersey. The principal actually hired someone to coach recess. The story warranted front page coverage in *The New York Times*.

It seems the school was having a problem with boys and girls running into each other, arguing over basketballs, and ignoring kids they didn't want to hang out with. In other words, the kids were just being kids.

So the school outlawed unauthorized activities like hop-scotch and replaced them with structured free time. The rule at Broadway Elementary School? No goofing around during playtime.

Back when I was a youngster, recess was the most wonderful time of the day. It was a chance to get lost in the honeysuckle patch behind Hope P. Sullivan Elementary School. It was a time for me to daydream. It was a time to play make-believe with my friends. It was a time to fall down and get dirty, to scrape elbows and knees. It was a time to learn the hard and fast lessons of life. There are winners. There are losers. Sometimes you get knocked down, but you have to dust yourself off and get right back up.

Those lessons were brought to the big screen a few years ago in the inspirational movie, *Dodgeball: A True Underdog Story*.[4] The film follows a band of misfits as they triumph over great obstacles and become dodgeball champions. Their winning mantra—dodge, duck, dip, dive, and dodge.

But dodgeball is now considered the sport of barbarians. We are a much more evolved people. I suppose we owe a debt of gratitude to the intellectual elites who got us into this predicament. But if you ask me, I think some of them forgot to dodge, duck, dip, dive, and dodge.

Pro-Gay or Anti-Straight?

 It's hard enough learning about the birds and bees; now American school children are going to have to learn about gay penguins. It's all part of a global effort to teach kids about homosexuality, using buzz words like *anti-bullying* and *tolerance*. But to many parents and teachers, it sounds like indoctrination.

Gary Marksbury is a history teacher at a California high school. He's one of the few teachers who believe schools should give parents more latitude to pull their children out of courses that offend their religious beliefs.

That's where the penguins come in. *And Tango Makes Three*. It's a story about a pair of male penguins who raise a baby penguin, and it's featured on elementary school bookshelves across the country, much to the outrage of moms and dads.

"In today's world," Marksbury told FOX News, "it seems like tolerance is a one-way street for some people, so if you don't like the idea of same-gender marriage, you are immediately labeled a bigot."[1]

The New York Times, our national newspaper of record, said anyone who does not support gay marriage is a bigot. Their declaration came after California voters rejected same-sex marriage.

The paper bashed Christians, conservatives, and heterosexuals in one fell swoop.[2]

"The most notable defeat for fairness was in California," the paper reported, "where right-wing forces led by the Mormon Church poured tens of millions of dollars into the campaign for Proposition 8—a measure to enshrine bigotry in the state's Constitution by preventing people of the same sex from marrying." The *Times* forgot to mention the tens of millions of dollars spent by the pro-homosexual lobby.

In Alameda, California, the school system adopted a curriculum to teach grade-schoolers about respecting gay and lesbian families and students. Teachers will begin using the words "gay" and "lesbian" in fourth-grade classrooms. Parents were beyond furious when the school board voted to require the classes, especially when they learned that moms and dads are not allowed to keep their children out of them.

But in the quest to be pro-gay, have schools become anti-straight?

Lawmakers in Sacramento passed a landmark bill that would require students to take mandatory gay history classes. Supporters say it's the only way to counter anti-gay stereotypes and beliefs that make children in those groups vulnerable to bullying and suicide.

If that's the case, then when will schools start offering mandatory *straight* history classes?

"We are second-class citizens, and children are listening,"[3] Democratic lawmaker Mark Leno told the Associated Press, defending the bill he sponsored. "When they see their teachers don't step up to the plate when their classmate is being harassed literally to death, they are listening and they get the message that there is something wrong with those people."

But opponents wonder why children so young would be required to contemplate sexuality, especially when many parents are teaching their kids abstinence.

As we say down South, I don't care how you butter your biscuit. This is a free country, and that means you're free to do as you want within the boundaries of the law. What I do in the privacy of my home is my business. And what you do in the privacy of your home is your business.

But it seems to me that some activists within the gay-rights movement are interested in something else. Special protection under the law is not good enough. They want to force you to change your way of thinking—twenty-first-century thought police. They want to attack religious beliefs that conflict with their own.

David Stockton learned this lesson the hard way. He is the owner of Just Cookies, a family bakery in Indianapolis. One day members of a gay-rights group asked Stockton to make a batch of rainbow-themed cupcakes for National Coming Out Day.

Stockton had two problems with the request. First, Stockton had reservations about what the group stood for. As he told a local television station, "We are a family business."[4] But there was also a second issue: Stockton doesn't make cupcakes. Hence the name of his store—Just Cookies.

Gay-rights groups went into crisis mode and immediately launched protests, accusing the bakery of discrimination. The mayor's office called the private company's actions "unacceptable." And the Office of Equal Opportunity launched an investigation.

The plight of the Stockton family has been felt across the country. Individuals who gave money to oppose gay marriage in California found their businesses protested. A waitress in one community was forced to quit her job after activists picketed the restaurant where she worked. Her crime was supporting the traditional definition of marriage.

On the following pages, you will read about real-life incidents where people who oppose gay marriage, gay parenting, and the normalization of the gay lifestyle have come under relentless attack.

Students Ordered to Attend Gay Seminar

A group of fourteen-year-old students at Deerfield High School in Illinois were ordered to attend a mandatory homosexual seminar. The class featured gay students talking about their personal experiences.

"This is unbelievable," said Matt Barber of Concerned Women for America. "It's not enough that students at Deerfield High are being exposed to improper and offensive material relative to unhealthy and high-risk homosexual behavior, but they've essentially been told by teachers to lie to their parents about it."[5] CWA called it a "shocking and brazen act of government abuse of parental rights," alleging students were told to sign confidentiality agreements—promising not to tell their parents about the seminar.

The *Chicago Tribune* reported that many parents were furious because religious groups opposed to homosexuality were denounced during the seminar's discussion time.

"This goes to the heart of the homosexual agenda," Barber told WorldNetDaily. "The professional propagandists in the 'gay-rights' lobby know the method all too well. If you can maintain control of undeveloped and impressionable youth and spoon-feed them misinformation, lies, and half-truths about dangerous, disordered, and extremely risky behaviors, then you can control the future and ensure that those behaviors are not only fully accepted, but celebrated."

Court: School Can Expel Student Who Opposes Homosexuality

A federal judge ruled in favor of a public university that removed a Christian student over her belief that homosexuality is morally wrong. The decision, according to Julea Ward's attorneys, could result in Christian students across the country being expelled from public universities for similar views.

"It's a dangerous precedent," said Jeremy Tedesco, legal

counsel for the conservative Alliance Defense Fund. "The ruling doesn't say that explicitly, but that's what is going to happen."

U.S. District Judge George Caram Steeh dismissed Ward's lawsuit against Eastern Michigan University. She was removed from the school's counseling program because she refused to counsel homosexual clients. The university contended she violated school policy and the American Counseling Association code of ethics.

"Christian students shouldn't be expelled for holding to and abiding by their beliefs," said ADF senior counsel David French. "To reach its decision, the court had to do something that's never been done in federal court: uphold an extremely broad and vague university speech code."

Eastern Michigan University hailed the decision.

"We are pleased that the court has upheld our position in this matter," EMU spokesman Walter Kraft said in a written statement. "Julea Ward was not discriminated against because of her religion. To the contrary, Eastern Michigan is deeply committed to the education of our students and welcomes individuals from diverse backgrounds into our community."

In his forty-eight-page opinion, Judge Steeh said the university had a rational basis for adopting the ACA Code of Ethics. "Furthermore, the university had a rational basis for requiring students to counsel clients without imposing their personal values,"[6] he wrote in a portion of his ruling posted by *The Detroit News*. "In the case of Ms. Ward, the university determined that she would never change her behavior and would consistently refuse to counsel clients on matters with which she was personally opposed due to her religious beliefs, including homosexual relationships."

Ward's attorneys claim the university told her she would only be allowed to remain in the program if she went through a "remediation" program so that she could "see the error of her ways" and change her belief system about homosexuality.

The case is similar to a lawsuit the ADF filed against Augusta State University in Georgia. Counseling student Jennifer Keeton was allegedly told to stop sharing her Christian beliefs in order to graduate.

Keeton's lawsuit alleged she was told to undergo a reeducation program and attend "diversity sensitivity training."

Tedesco said both cases should be a warning to Christians attending public colleges and universities. "Public universities are imposing the ideological stances of private groups on their students," he said. "If you don't comply, you will be kicked out. It's scary stuff, and it's not a difficult thing to see what's coming down the pike."

Christian Beauty Queens versus Gays

In the beginning there was Carrie Prejean, the former Miss California USA who was castigated by the anti-straight media for her opposition to gay marriage. Now activists are setting their sights on Miss Beverly Hills, Lauren Ashley.

Ashley was a contestant in the Miss California USA pageant. She came under assault for her belief that marriage should be between a man and a woman.

"I feel like God himself created mankind and he loves everyone, and he has the best for everyone,"[7] she told FOX News. "If he says that having sex with someone of your same gender is going to bring death upon you, that's a pretty stern warning, and he knows more than we do about life."

Before you could take a commercial break, the anti-straight crowd assembled torches and pitchforks. Perez Hilton proclaimed on his entertainment Web site, "There's a new dumb [bleep] in town."[8] Others called her anti-gay, a Christian homophobe. Her fate was similar to Carrie Prejean, who lost her beauty crown because she said gays should not be allowed to marry.

But Ashley's case took a few unusual turns. The pageant director, who is gay, supported his beauty queen. "I don't agree with her, but I will fight to the death for her right to have her opinion,"[9] Keith Lewis told the *Los Angeles Times*.

The other issue had to do with her residency. It turns out the pageant does not require the contestant to live in the city she is representing. Ashley lived in Pasadena, not Beverly Hills. Well, that flew all over the mayor who issued a press release saying they were dismayed and shocked at any potential association with Ashley and the city of Beverly Hills. The mayor said they have a history of tolerance and respect (as long as you aren't a born-again Christian who opposes same-sex marriage, apparently).

Seven-Year-Olds Take Field Trip to Gay District

Should little boys be exposed to a section of town where grown men frolic in the nude? That seems to be the genesis of a controversy in San Francisco involving a private, all-boys school sponsoring a day trip to the Castro, the city's world-renowned gay district. The neighborhood includes pornographic shops with window displays and all sorts of unmentionable gadgets. It's sort of like a grown-up perverted Chuck E. Cheese.

But was it age appropriate for the four dozen second-graders from the Town School? The mother of one little boy reached out to the local CBS television station. "Why would you talk to a young child about sex with a man and a woman, let alone a man and a man or a woman and a woman?" the woman asked. "It just doesn't seem right. They are not ready for that."

The *San Francisco Chronicle* reported that other parents were upset because teachers told the students the word *gay* means "happy."[10] I wonder how they defined the word *straight?*

The school defended the trip and said it was a great success, intended to expose children to different perspectives and views. But one parent told the newspaper she was worried about what else the children may have been exposed to. "I know that Castro is full of regular shops and restaurants, but I also know that there are lots of shops with neon signs and windows that display things that, well, I just don't need more questions about!" the parent wrote. "I would not be OK with a tour of North Beach either that included certain streets. So I don't think this is a gay issue."

Librarian Forced Out by Anti-Gay Book

A federal judge has tossed out a lawsuit filed by a former Ohio State University librarian who said he was forced out of his job because of his conservative Christian beliefs. U.S. District Court Judge William Bertelsman ruled that the university's Mansfield campus did not violate Scott Savage's civil rights by being hostile to his beliefs.

In 2006 Savage was asked to serve on a committee to develop a required reading list for incoming freshmen. He noticed that every book was either liberal or promoted what he called a gay agenda. So Savage recommended four conservative books, and that's where his troubles began.

According to the court ruling, one of the books, *The Marketing of Evil*,[11] contained a chapter discussing homosexuality as "aberrant human behavior." Several professors on the committee immediately took offense, accusing Savage of recommending a "homophobic book."

Two professors were so upset over the book that they filed a sexual-discrimination complaint against Savage. But the attack against Savage didn't stop there.

According to *The Columbus Dispatch*, English professor J. F. Buckley wrote an e-mail and sent it to the entire faculty.[12] Buckley wrote: "You have made me fearful and uneasy being a gay man on this campus . . . I no longer feel safe doing my job. I am being harassed."

WorldNetDaily reported Savage received other correspondence laced with curse words and vicious personal attacks.[13] The Christian librarian was later publicly condemned by a faculty vote.

"Rather than being examples of how I am 'provoking controversy,' these incidents underline the growing intolerance toward our constitutional rights on many campuses," Savage wrote in a letter that was published May 13, 2006, in *The Dispatch*.

Savage then accused five faculty members of falsely accusing him of harassment. But in 2007, he said he was forced to leave his job because of what he called personal and professional attacks on his character.

OSU is "an aggressive proponent of the homosexual lifestyle by virtue of its practices and policies," he said in the lawsuit. "OSU is therefore a naturally hostile environment to the expression of traditional Christian beliefs and morality."

But Judge Bertelsman said that Savage's speech was not protected by the First Amendment. He also ruled that the professors who launched the complaints were not in a position to discipline him and that he had his supervisor's support.

Anti-Gay Couple Denied Foster Children

A British court has ruled that a Christian couple can no longer care for foster children because of their opposition to homosexuality. Eunice and Owen Johns provided foster care for nearly two dozen children in the 1990s, but after Great Britain instituted equality laws, they were banned from the program in 2007.

Social workers red-flagged the couple during an interview when they explained they did not approve of homosexuality because of their Pentecostal faith. The Associated Press reported that judges at London's Royal Courts of Justice determined that laws protecting homosexuals from discrimination take precedence over the couple's religious beliefs.[14] Britain, the judges ruled, was a "secular state, not a theocracy."

The Johns told the *Press and Journal* newspaper they were "extremely distressed."

"We have been excluded because we have moral opinions based on our faith, and we feel sidelined because we are Christians with normal, mainstream views on sexual ethics," Mrs. Johns said.

British gay-rights organizations praised the ruling. "In any fostering case, the interests of the 60,000 children in care should override the bias of any prospective parent," gay-rights activist Ben Summerskill told *Pink News*, Europe's largest gay news service.[15] "Thankfully Mr. and Mrs. Johns's outdated views aren't just out of step with the majority of people in modern Britain but those of many Christians, too."

Meanwhile, this particular battle in the culture war has even influenced a flavor of ice cream. Ben and Jerry's celebrated the start of legalized gay marriage in Vermont by offering a limited-edition brand of ice cream, renaming Chubby Hubby to Hubby, Hubby. The New England ice cream maker wanted to herald wedded bliss with peace, love, and ice cream.

If it's not too much trouble, I'll just take a scoop of vanilla, please.

Dispatches from the Pew

3❍

The War on Christianity

In 2007, then Senator Barack Obama told the Christian Broadcasting Network that the United States was "no longer just a Christian nation." But a new Gallup poll indicates that not only is the country Christian; it is *overwhelmingly* Christian.

Somebody better alert the White House. They've got a Christian nation on their hands.

According to Gallup, 78 percent of Americans consider themselves Christian. Breaking down the numbers, we find 56 percent of Americans identify themselves Protestant and 22 percent Catholic.[1]

But there's trouble brewing across the fruited plain. Activist judges and public school systems have declared a war on Christianity. The basic tenets of our faith are under attack. And it's pretty clear a majority of the country understands what's happening.

Rasmussen Reports released a poll showing 64 percent of Americans believe judges are anti-religious. Among evangelical Christians that number soars to 87 percent.[2]

"Legal scholars, religious leaders, and politicians have argued for decades over whether the 'separation of church and state' is actually enshrined in the Constitution," the report stated. "One side argues that the Constitution merely prohibits the establishment of a government-mandated official religion, but the other reads in the document the complete banishment of religion from anything touched by the government. The courts in recent years have leaned in the direction of the latter position."

The Rasmussen findings were released after a federal judge ruled the National Day of Prayer statute was unconstitutional. The Rasmussen poll also found that 46 percent believe the Supreme Court has been too hostile toward religion; only 13 percent said it has been too friendly toward religion.

As you've read in these pages, federal judges have also banned religious activities in school and even outlawed the playing of Christmas carols with religious lyrics.

In 2009 the Third U.S. Circuit Court of Appeals ruled that a kindergartner's mother could not read Scripture during show-and-tell at her child's school, even though it was the boy's favorite book.

In Marietta, Georgia, city officials considered changing the oath police officers take to remove the phrase "so help me God."

Perhaps one of the most disgusting anti-Christian rulings came from the courtroom of Judge M. Casey Rodgers. The Florida judge ruled the Santa Rosa School District was well within its rights to crack down on Christian teachers. The order prevents teachers from praying, reading their Bibles, or even responding to e-mail from parents that might include the words "God bless you."

During court testimony one teacher described how she was forced to hide behind a closet door to pray with a colleague whose two-year-old child had died.

Need more proof that Christianity is being marginalized and, in some cases, placed under outright attack? Just check out these dispatches:

Democrat Wants Capitol Prayers, Pastor Banned

A Minnesota lawmaker wants state senate leaders to order chaplains to keep their senate invocations nondenominational and refrain from overt mentions of Jesus, Christianity, or any other faith-specific references.

State Senator Terri Bonoff, who is Jewish, said she feels uncomfortable when ministers mention Jesus and Christianity during prayers.

The breaking point came when Dennis Campbell, the pastor of Granite City Baptist Church, offered a prayer that mentioned Jesus Christ three times. "And we pray, Lord, that you help us to show reverence to the Lord Jesus Christ and the word of God today," Campbell prayed.

After the prayer Bonoff rose to voice her objections. She also demanded he not be invited back. And now the Democratic lawmaker wants senate leaders to require chaplains to deliver nondenominational prayers.

"I'm a religious woman and believe deeply in God," Bonoff told Twincities.com. "We honor God in public and our political discourse, and that's proper. But in doing a nondenominational prayer we are honoring him without violating the separation of church and state."[3]

State Senator David Brown, who invited Pastor Campbell to the senate, defended the prayer. "If we're going to invite clergy to the Senate session to pray, we know they're coming from a denomination or a religion that represents a belief system," he said. "I believe we don't have the right to censor their prayers."

Child Banned from Passing Out Party Invitations

A Pennsylvania elementary school that prohibited a student from inviting classmates to a church Christmas party is now the focus of a discrimination lawsuit filed in federal court. The Alliance Defense Fund (ADF) filed the suit against the Pocono Mountain School District on behalf of a fifth-grade student. The student claims she was not allowed to pass out fliers inviting Barrett Elementary Center students to a party at her church.

District policies, according to ADF attorney David Cortman, prohibit any student speech promoting Christianity. "It's another example where schools need to be educated about the First Amendment," Cortman said. "The policies that are at the heart of this lawsuit are unconstitutional."

A spokesperson for the Pocono Mountain School District said they were not aware of the lawsuit and would be unable to comment on any pending litigation.

Cortman said the incident in question occurred when the child tried to distribute the fliers before class started. The twenty-eight-page lawsuit only identifies the student by her initials, "K.A." and refers to her as a Christian who "desires to share her religious views with her classmates."

According to the lawsuit, the church Christmas party was not overtly religious. It invited children to participate in "face painting, ping-pong, foosball," along with refreshments.

"The teacher said she needed to get permission from the principal, so she went to the principal, who then said she needed to get permission from the superintendent," Cortman said. "The superintendent denied her request."

Cortman said the irony is that students are allowed to distribute fliers and invitations for nonreligious events all the time. "Other students can hand out fliers for birthday parties, pizza parties, and Halloween parties," he said. "In this case, because it was religious, it was denied."

Fellowship of Christian Athletes Told to Take Down Religious Posters

A group of Christian athletes in Virginia is taking a stand against their high school after administrators tore down copies of the Ten Commandments posted on their lockers. Officials at Floyd County High School reportedly told the students only secular messages like "Happy Birthday" or "Go Team" are allowed on lockers.

The students are members of the Fellowship of Christian Athletes. When the Ten Commandments were removed from their lockers, they contacted the Liberty Counsel, a legal firm promoting religious freedom.

"These acts of censorship violate the students' right to free speech," said Liberty Counsel founder Mathew Staver. "In this case the school has opened up student lockers for student expression and is monitoring and censoring religious speech."

Staver sent a letter to Barry Hollandsworth, principal of the high school, asking that the students be allowed to repost the Ten Commandments. The school did not return phone calls seeking comment.

In a rare turn of events, the Virginia chapter of the American Civil Liberties Union is also supporting the students. "Schools have the authority to ban all displays on school property," wrote ACLU of Virginia Executive Director Kent Willis in a press release. "But if a school allows students to post some kinds of personal messages on their lockers, it must also allow other kinds of messages, including those that have religious content."

Lawsuit Filed against Woman
Who Wanted Christian Roommate

A civil rights complaint has been filed against a Grand Rapids woman who posted an advertisement at her church last July seeking a Christian roommate. "The statement expresses an illegal preference for a Christian roommate, thus excluding people of other faiths," according to the complaint filed by the Fair Housing Center of West Michigan.

"It's a violation to make, print or publish a discriminatory statement," Executive Director Nancy Haynes told FOX News. "There are no exemptions to that."[4]

Haynes said the unnamed thirty-one-year-old woman's alleged violation was turned over to the Michigan Department of Civil Rights. Depending on the outcome of her case, the Christian woman could face several hundreds of dollars in fines and "fair housing training so it doesn't happen again."

"This is outrageous," said attorney Joel Oster, with the Alliance Defense Fund. His organization is representing the woman free of charge. "Clearly this woman has a right to pick and choose who she wants to live with." Oster said he's sent a letter to the state asking them to dismiss the case as groundless.

"Christians shouldn't live in fear of being punished by the government for being Christians," he said. "It is completely absurd to try to penalize a single Christian woman for privately seeking a Christian roommate at church, an obviously legal and constitutionally protected activity."

But Haynes said they plan on pursuing the matter. "We want to make sure it doesn't happen again," she said.

The person who filed the initial complaint apparently saw the ad on the church bulletin board. It included the words, "Christian roommate wanted" along with her contact information. Had the ad not included the word "Christian," she said it would not have been illegal.

"If you read it and you were not Christian, would you not feel welcome to rent there?" Haynes asked.

But isn't that the point?

And that, said Haynes, is discrimination.

Oster said he hopes the case will eventually be dropped. "The First Amendment guarantees us freedom of religion," he said. "And we have the right to live with someone of the same faith. The Michigan Department of Civil Rights is denying her rights by pursuing this complaint."

Catholic Professor Fired for Teaching Catholic Doctrine

A professor at the University of Illinois has been fired for teaching Catholic doctrine in a class about Catholic doctrine and was subsequently accused by a student of engaging in hate speech.

Dr. Ken Howell was on the faculty at the university for nine years. He was removed from the classroom after he told students he agreed with the Catholic Church's teaching that homosexual sex is immoral.

"The facts are quite simple," said attorney Travis Barham. "Dr. Howell has been relieved because he taught Catholic doctrine in a class about Catholic doctrine." Barham is with Alliance Defense Fund and will be representing the fired professor.

"As absurd as it sounds, those are the facts," Barham told FOX News Radio. "This should be disturbing not just for Catholics or Evangelicals but for everyone who cares about free speech."[5]

Barham said the university cannot censor a professor's speech just because someone finds it offensive. "It's profoundly disturbing. You have a professor who was removed from the classroom because someone found his speech offensive," Barham said.

Howell's firing has generated outrage on campus and among the nation's Catholics.

"Codes of academic freedom were written expressly to combat abuses like this, and that is why this case must be taken seriously," said Bill Donohue, president of the Catholic League. "He was fired for his religious viewpoint, an unacceptable reason that will not stand up in court."

Pastor Fired as Chaplain for Jesus Prayer

A North Carolina pastor was relieved of his duties as an honorary chaplain of the state House of Representatives after he closed a prayer by invoking the name of Jesus.

Ron Baity, pastor of Berean Baptist Church in Winston-Salem, was invited to lead prayer in the legislative chamber for an entire week, but his tenure was cut short when he refused to remove the name of Jesus from his invocation.

Baity's troubles began when a house clerk asked to see his prayer. "The invocation included prayers for our military, state lawmakers, and a petition to God asking him to bless North Carolina.

"When I handed it to the lady, I watched her eyes, and they immediately went right to the bottom of the page and the word *Jesus*," he recalled. "She said, 'We would prefer that you not use the name Jesus. We have some people here that can be offended.'"

When Baity protested, the clerk brought the matter to the attention of House Speaker Joe Hackney. "I told her I was highly offended when she asked me not to pray in the name of Jesus because that does constitute my faith," Baity said. "My faith requires that I pray in His name. The Bible is clear."

When the clerk returned, Baity said he was told that he would be allowed to deliver the day's prayer, but after that his services would no longer be needed.

"When the state tells you how to pray, that you cannot use the name of Jesus, that's mandating a state religion," he said. "They talk about not offending other people but at the same time, if they are telling me how to pray, that's the thing our forefathers left England for."

The Christian Law Association helped Baity draft a letter asking for an apology and an opportunity to return to the state capitol and finish his tenure.

"The First Amendment promises all Americans the free exercise of their religion, which includes the right to pray as their faith requires, even when they are invited to open state legislative sessions with prayer,"[6] attorney David Gibbs told WXII-TV. "We trust that the North Carolina House of Representatives will realize its mistake and will offer Pastor Baity another opportunity to pray without requiring him to use a prayer that is mandated by the government."

Baity said he is still stunned by what happened. "You would expect this somewhere else—Cuba, Saudi Arabia," he said. "You would never anticipate this happening in the United States of America." In a word, the pastor said, the decision is "anti-Christian."

In the Year of Our Lord—Unconstitutional

When high school seniors in New Haven, Connecticut, receive their diplomas this week, they will not be graduating "in the year of our Lord." The school district has removed the traditional phrase from high school diplomas after someone complained.

"It's a religious thing," Superintendent Reginald Mayo told the *New Haven Register*. "I'm surprised it took this long for someone to notice it. We certainly don't want to offend anyone."[7]

"This is political correctness gone mad," said Bill Donohue, president of the Catholic League. "What this New Haven school is doing is more than a detour from our moorings; it is unconscionable. Attempts to scrub clean any reference to our founding is a disservice to the students and their community."

Last year former alderwoman Ina Silverman filed a complaint about "in the year of our Lord." Her daughter was a student at Wilbur Cross High School. According to the newspaper, she took her concerns to the mayor, who then asked the superintendent to censor the words.

Mayo told the newspaper it was a small but necessary change. The American Humanist Association heralded the decision.

"It removes the bias toward Christianity and puts all New Haven students on an equal plain without religious bias," said Bob Ritter, a staff lawyer with the American Humanist Association. "The fact of the matter is all New Haven students deserve a diploma which is religiously neutral. It favors no religion over another."

But some Christians disagree with that assessment. Local resident Betsy Claro called the decision "hideous."

"I do believe that it's a travesty to keep removing the Lord's name," the mother of three told me. "Our nation was founded on the principles of belief in God, and our founding fathers made sure it was incorporated into every document they produced."

It's not the first time the phrase has generated controversy. A Muslim student at Trinity University in San Antonio petitioned to have the words removed from diplomas. That university, affiliated with the Presbyterian Church of America, decided to keep the wording in place.

High School Ordered to End Pre-Game Prayers

A Wisconsin-based, freedom-from-religion group has accused a Tennessee high school of violating the civil rights of students by allowing someone to pray before Friday night football games. And now the Freedom from Religion Foundation is demanding Soddy-Daisy High School end the prayers or else. The group sent a letter to local school officials demanding an immediate end to the football prayers, as well as prayers delivered at the high school graduation ceremony.

"The prayers before the Soddy-Daisy High School football games constitute an unconstitutional government endorsement of religion," wrote attorney Rebecca Markert in a letter to Hamilton County School Superintendent Jim Scales. She called the prayers a "serious and flagrant violation of the First Amendment."

The Wisconsin group said they were representing "concerned" students. A spokesperson for the school system declined to comment because their attorney was out of town. Board of Education member Rhonda Thurman, however, told the *Chattanooga Times Free Press* the prayers were a longstanding tradition.[8]

She suggested people who didn't want to listen to the prayer should "put their fingers in their ears." Some local residents said they were offended by the accusations.

"I think Wisconsin ought to take care of Wisconsin," Rhonda Jewell told FOX. "We are in the Bible Belt. Prayer is an accepted practice, and they should just leave us alone."[9]

Parent Jim Rogers told the *Chattanooga Times Free Press* that he believes public prayer is a protected form of speech. "People who find Christianity contrary to their beliefs shouldn't be offended that [Christians] have the freedom to express their religious beliefs," he said.

The group has given the school system several weeks to respond to their letter. What happens if they don't is unclear.

Annie Laurie Gaylor, a copresident of the foundation, told the newspaper the school had "no leg to stand on."

"Students are a captive audience; they're required to go to school," she said. "When there is a violation like a prayer at a school, they're really vulnerable; it's a violation of their civil rights."

Punished for Talking about Jesus

A Wisconsin teenager was sent to the principal's office for talking about Jesus. Nathan De La Garza was having a conversation with another student about the Bible during free time at Park High School in Racine, Wisconsin. A teacher overheard him and told him he wasn't allowed to talk about religion. The following day Nathan was sent to the principal's office.

According to *The Journal Times*, Nathan said the principal told him "in a nice way" to stop talking about religion during class and "to keep it to lunch and out of school."[10] The principal said he might offend somebody, and they might start a fight with him. "The last thing we want," Nathan said she told him, "is for you to get into a fight about God."

Nathan, who attends a local Assembly of God church, said he was encouraged by his youth pastor to carry his Bible wherever he goes, and he's more than happy to speak with other students about religion. "The atheist people, they try ganging up on you all the time," he told the newspaper. "They make the rudest comments."

His private comments about Christianity led to his trip to the principal's office. The school district said students are allowed to carry Bibles but are not allowed to be disruptive. Nathan said he was in no way disruptive.

Thou Shalt Not Pray

A group of elderly residents at a Dallas public housing project have been ordered by the government to shut down their church. The Dallas Housing Authority said the services violate the U.S. Constitution and the agency's contract with the U.S. Department of Housing and Urban Development.

"It's all federal money, so we're subject to constitutional prohibitions," DHA president MaryAnn Russ told *The Dallas Morning News*. "It's like prayer in public schools. It's the same deal."[11]

But a HUD spokesman said the Fair Housing Act does not prohibit religious activity in common areas of public housing.

My goodness, the Lake Highlands United Methodist Church has been conducting the worship services at the housing project for about fourteen years. Many of those attending are elderly and unable to drive to other churches.

"It's just something we will miss terribly," eighty-four-year-old Myrna Hardy told the newspaper. "It's like putting a big hole in our lives."

A similar tradition came to an end in Port Wentworth, Georgia, too. Senior citizens who eat their meals at the local senior center were ordered to stop praying over the food. Instead, the elderly were told they could only take part in a moment of silence.

The meals are provided by a group called Senior Citizens, Inc. Officials said they are just following guidelines determined by the federal government.

Tim Rutherford, a vice president of the organization, told WSB-TV that since the meals are mostly funded by tax dollars, there's a separation of church-state issue at play. "We can't scoff at their rules," he told the television station. "It's part of the operational guidelines."[12]

Rutherford stressed they weren't forbidding people to pray—just out loud. "We're asking them to pray to themselves," he told WSB. "Have that moment of silence."

As you might imagine, folks in Port Wentworth, located in the heart of the Bible Belt, are outraged.

Mayor Glenn "Pig" Jones had to deliver the news to the elderly residents of his town, calling it one of the hardest things he's ever had to do. "For me to look at their eyes and tell them they can't thank God for their food—it's unheard of—I can't take it,"[13] he told the *Savannah Morning News*.

As one elderly lady said, the government may be able to stop her from speaking, but they can't stop her from praying what's in her heart.

University Says Christianity Is Oppressive

More than two dozen Christian students at the University of California at Davis have filed a formal complaint over a university policy that defines religious discrimination as Christians oppressing non-Christians. The definition is listed in a document called "The Principles of Community." It defines "Religious/Spiritual Discrimination" as "the loss of power and privilege to those who do not practice the dominant culture's religion. In the United States, this is institutionalized oppressions toward those who are not Christian."

"This is radical political correctness run amok," said David French, senior counsel for the Alliance Defense Fund. The conservative advocacy group has written a letter on behalf of more than twenty-five students who object to the policy and want it revised. He said it's absurd to single out Christians as oppressors and non-Christians as the only oppressed people on campus.

"Christians deserve the same protections against religious discrimination as any other students on a public university campus," French told me. "The idea that a university would discriminate against Christians is an old story, unfortunately, and one that we see played out every day."

One student, who asked not to be identified, said university officials asked her to reaffirm "The Principles of Community" last semester. She refused to do so when she realized Christians were not protected under the policy.

"To have a nondiscrimination policy that excludes the Christian faith is a cause for action," she said. "In higher academia, one would hope that a diversity of ideas and beliefs would be appreciated. But my experience has been that this has not always been the case. There is a real fear of bias against the Christian faith."

French said all students who complained are fearful of backlash if their identities became known.

"This was amazing to actually enshrine in your nondiscrimination statement—discrimination against Christians," he said. "This is a symbol of the seeming impunity in which universities violate the law to establish a radical, secular-left agenda."

Alan Brownstein, a law professor at UC-Davis, said the campus has a generally open and tolerant view of religion. "It's a university campus," he said. "There is robust debate and people will disagree on just about everything."

Brownstein, who is a nationally known constitutional scholar, said any legal challenges to the policy would depend on whether it's a binding document.

"Clearly, if you had an enforceable regulatory policy that said, 'We will discipline Christians who oppress non-Christians, but we will not impose the same kind of disciplinary sanctions on non-Christians who engage in the same kind of harassing behavior against Christians,' that would be unacceptable and subject to legal challenge."

Regardless, Brownstein said it might have been more appropriate to use less specific language in the policy. "It's always preferable to be as general as you can when you describe these kinds of unacceptable behaviors," he said.

Vets Defy Order to Remove Christian Flag

A Christian flag is once again flying at a Veteran's Memorial in King, North Carolina, in defiance of a decision made by town leaders facing a possible lawsuit. A group of military veterans erected the flag on a temporary stand and have vowed to stand guard twenty-four hours a day, daring anyone to try to take it down.

"It's gonna stay here as long as I can stand," said Ray Martini in an interview with the *Winston-Salem Journal*. "We're going to stand watch and guard it twenty-four hours a day, seven days a week."[14]

The King Police Department said the group can keep the flag at the memorial but only if someone is with the flag at all times.

"I refuse to let a few turn around and try to desecrate our intensive fighting and defending of America by taking down what the majority love," Martini told WGHP-TV. "If you don't like what we've done here, then just don't come."[15]

The decision to remove the flag stems from estimates that it could cost the city as much as $300,000 to fight a possible lawsuit from the ACLU. The controversy started when an Afghanistan war veteran complained about the Christian flag being flown at the memorial.

City officials took it down on the advice of their attorney, who said it violated the First Amendment. The city had also received letters from several advocacy groups threatening lawsuits; among those groups was Americans United for the Separation of Church and State. "They have done the right thing," executive director Barry Lynn told the newspaper. "It would be unfortunate if they reversed their decision."

After the flag was removed, the same veteran demanded the city remove a cross from another monument showing a soldier kneeling next to a grave.

"We aren't going to lay down for this," Jim Rasmond told the newspaper. "I don't believe in one person telling all of us what to do."

Meanwhile, Christian flag sales are booming. Several hundred have been sold in the small town, and local sentiment is overwhelmingly on the side of the Christian flag and cross.

"It is time for Christians to stand up to the ACLU and not be strong-armed by the ACLU," resident Michael Lane told the newspaper. "It is our constitutional right to fly a Christian flag on public or private property."

Professor Compares Crucifix to Swastika

Eastfield College is accused of suppressing the religious expression of students after a ceramics instructor compared the crucifix to a swastika and refused to allow students to create religious symbols.

"Unfortunately, not everyone has the Christmas spirit or even a basic understanding of religious freedom," Kelly Shackelford, chief counsel of Liberty Legal Institute, said in a statement. "The government cannot ban crosses and religious symbols."

The controversy involves retired auto worker Joe Mitchell and Eastfield Community College in Mesquite, Texas. Since 2006, he has been enrolled in a noncredit ceramics class comprised mostly of retirees. During the spring class, Mitchell made a number of crosses for friends and fellow parishioners at St. Bernard of Clairvaux Catholic Church.

That's when he ran into trouble. According to court documents, a memorandum was sent to students forbidding them from creating any religious items including those representing Christmas and Easter.

"The making of such pieces at Eastfield College demeans the goals of the ceramic program at EFC," stated a memo written by James Watral, chair of the ceramics program.

Mitchell filed a complaint with the college, alleging they were discriminating against people of faith. The college apologized and offered an amended rule that prohibited replicas of religious items. But last fall Mitchell ran afoul of the school once again when an instructor questioned whether he would be creating any religiously themed work.

Here's what happened next, according to the Liberty Legal

Institute: "Ms. Blackhurst then asked Mr. Mitchell if he considered a swastika offensive. He responded, 'Of course.' She then proceeded to compare the cross to a swastika. She stated that many individuals view the cross as an offensive symbol in the same way many people are offended by swastikas, and that his crosses would therefore not be fired by the department."

"I felt humiliated and that my spirituality was being demeaned," Mitchell said in a written statement. "The whole point of art is to express who you are."

"It appears the Eastfield College art department has no room in the inn for artistic religious expression such as that of Michelangelo or Leonardo da Vinci; hopefully they will change their minds," said Hiram Sasser, director of litigation at Liberty Legal Institute.

Third-Grader Barred from Reading Bible

A New Jersey third-grader broke down in tears after a teacher told the girl her Bible was not appropriate reading material for a public school. After a public uproar the principal of the school apologized to Mariah Jordat and told her it was all a misunderstanding.

Michelle Jordat said her daughter loves the Bible and was hurt when the teacher told her to pack away her Bible during quiet reading time. "This was injustice," she said. "No other child has to go through this again."

The school said the teacher made a mistake and that school policy does allow children to read the Bible or any other religious book during reading time.

Child Who Drew Jesus Ordered to See Shrink

A school superintendent in Taunton, Massachusetts, has been ordered to apologize to the family of an eight-year-old boy who was sent home from school and ordered to undergo a psychiatric evaluation after drawing a picture of Jesus on a cross.

"The mayor is upset and angry," said Todd Castro, assistant to Mayor Charles Crowley. "He spoke with the superintendent this morning and is looking for her to make a public apology and a private apology to the family."

According to the *Taunton Daily Gazette*, a boy at Maxham Elementary School was instructed to sketch something that reminded him of Christmas.[16] The child had just returned from a visit to the National Shrine of Our Lady of La Salette, so he drew a stick figure of Jesus on the cross.

The boy's father, who asked not to be identified, told the newspaper he received a call from the school telling him his son had created a violent drawing. "As far as I'm concerned, they're violating his religion," he said.

He was referred by a mutual friend to Toni Saunders, an educational consultant who helps children with special needs. "The father was so angry at what had happened to his son," she said. "It didn't make sense to him."

Bill Donohue, president of the Catholic League, told me: "We're going to question the mental state of the child for simply drawing a picture of Christ crucified? There's something serious going on at this school."

Giving Kids Bibles Is Against the Law

Giving away Bibles to schoolchildren is unconstitutional. That's the law of the land in Wilson County, Tennessee, a suburb of Nashville. The school board was facing a lawsuit from the American Civil Liberties Union over a longtime tradition.

Every year fifth-grade students were presented free Bibles from The Gideons International. The Gideons are based in Nashville and have been giving away pocket-sized copies of The New Testament, Proverbs, and Psalms for decades. Last year they distributed more than eleven million Bibles.

Boys and girls in Wilson County were not required to take the Bibles, but the parents of one child complained. They admit their daughter was not forced to accept the Bible, but the girl was afraid of being singled out for ridicule had she refused.

That's when the ACLU got involved. "Decisions about religion should be left in the hands of families and faith communities, not public school officials,"[17] said ACLU attorney Edmund J. Schmidt III in an interview with *The Tennessean*.

The ACLU demanded the school district stop giving away Bibles on school grounds. To avoid a lawsuit, school officials were forced not only to ban God's Word but also to acknowledge that giving kids a Bible on school property is unconstitutional.

The ACLU of Tennessee hailed the ruling and said their goal is to protect the religious liberty of everyone. Everyone, it seems, except Christians.

Dear Jesus, Will You Be My Facebook Friend?

 I recently informed the family that I have taken up twittering. My Aunt Lynn immediately had me placed on the church prayer list.

I tried to explain to her that Twitter is an online form of social networking—a sort of microblog that condenses one's thoughts into 140-character nuggets. But she was not convinced and warned me God-fearing Christians should not Twitter, especially in public.

Sadly, she may have a point. It seems churches across the country have not only *embraced* technology but in some ways are *worshipping* technology. Don't get me wrong: technology is great. I love air-conditioning and electricity. I have a laptop and a Blackberry. It's how the church is *using* technology that is up for discussion. There's a cottage industry of sanctified software catering to Christians seeking a digital deity.

A growing number of megachurch pastors are beaming their faces into churches hundreds of miles away, in essence becoming binary bishops. These cyberspace shepherds tend to their flocks in virtual reality churches.

"We live in a day and age and a culture where people go to school online, bank online, date online, and do other things online," said Kurt Ervin, who oversees the Internet campus for Central Christian Church in Henderson, Nevada. "Why not create a platform for them to go to church online?"[1]

Consider the following:

- One of the largest churches in the country is online. LifeChurch.tv broadcasts more than two dozen online services each week. The services attract up to sixty thousand unique views a week.
- At Flamingo Road Church in Florida, viewers can accept Jesus Christ as their Lord and Savior by clicking a tab. "The goal is to not let people at home feel like they're watching what's happening, but they're part of it," Rev. Brian Vasil told the Associated Press. "They're participating."
- The folks at Information Age Prayer have launched a Web site that prays to a variety of deities. For a monthly fee the company will arrange for a computer to intercede on your behalf. The most popular prayer package will set you back $4.95. It includes a Hail Mary, the Lord's Prayer, and whatever else floats your spiritual boat. They'll even throw in a Prayer for the Dead, depending on how your day's been going.
- Catholics are now able to confess their sins without going into a confessional booth. The Catholic Church signed off on an iPhone app that allows the faithful to confess their sins online. But they still have to visit a priest for absolution. Personally, I'm a PC guy—after what happened to Eve and the apple.
- Trinity Church, an Episcopal congregation in New York City, celebrated the Passion of the Tweet. The church literally presented a three-hour Passion Play online, continually tweeting the entire Easter story in bursts of 140 characters or less.

- Evangelist Chris Juby decided there was a market for a "shorter, punchier" version of the Good Book. So he decided to summarize the entire Bible in a series of daily tweets. Now, that's quite a challenge due to Twitter's word limit. And there are no exceptions. God may forgive seventy times seven but even *His* tweets are limited to seventy times two. I mean, "Jesus wept" is well within Twitter's guidelines, but what about all those passages where folks are "begetting" folks? Does tweeting, "@ Adam had a boatload of kids" really do justice to the Scriptures? Juby told AOL News that he was having a tough time condensing the Bible. "There's loads of really important stuff in there that I can't possibly convey on Twitter," he said. "Could I do justice to the 176 verses of Psalm 119 in 140 characters? Probably not."[2]

The other day I was pondering the Christian's responsibility in our computer-driven society when I received an e-mail from Cousin Billy. He could hardly contain his excitement.

"I just got a Facebook friend request from God," he wrote. "Can you believe it?"

I was a bit suspicious until I checked out God's Facebook page. It certainly seemed legitimate. He had several billion friends, listing Amy Grant and Michael W. Smith as His favorite musicians. Among His favorite books were the Bible and "anything written by Billy Graham." Under hobbies He wrote, "Creating things." As for His religious preference, He wrote, "Me."

A few minutes later Billy sent a Facebook friend request on my behalf to God, along with the Holy Spirit and Jesus. Sure enough God and the Holy Spirit became my friends, but there was an issue with Jesus. He declined my Facebook friend request. I was stunned. Why wouldn't Jesus accept my request?

"Maybe you should just poke Him," Billy suggested.

"Poke" Him. This is apparently a Facebook strategy for getting someone's attention. I decided that was not a good idea. There are a few unspoken rules in this world. Don't tug on Superman's cape and never try to poke Jesus.

I was really depressed. God was my Facebook friend, I was getting poked by the Holy Spirit, but Jesus was still ignoring my calls. I mean, He sits at the right hand of the Father. You'd think they would suggest friends to each other.

But a few days later I received an e-mail from Twitter that lifted my spirits. While the Lord ignored my Facebook friend request, He did want to become a follower of mine on Twitter.

I was so overjoyed, I wrote a song:

What a tweep we have in Jesus
All our sins and griefs to share
A hundred forty words should do it
If there's more I'd turn to prayer.

The other day Cousin Billy was visiting on a college break, and the conversation turned to Twitter. I proudly showed him Jesus was one of my followers.

"Uh, Todd, you might want to look at this," Billy said as he looked at my Twitter list. "I don't think Jesus is actually following you on Facebook."

I told Billy he was mistaken. I was following Jesus, and He was following me.

"No, really," he said. "You should check this out for yourself."

I glanced down the list of followers, and sure enough there was the name of Jesus.

"But check out the last name," Billy said.

I scrolled over to the profile page, and immediately I was crestfallen.

It was true. Jesus was indeed following me, but I'm afraid something got lost in translation. His last name wasn't Christ. It was Lopez.

And if that wasn't bad enough, I picked up a virus on my hard drive from one of those social networking sites.

Aunt Lynn is probably going to put me back on the church prayer list.

32

Gird Your Loins, the Preacher's Talking about Sex

In their quest to become culturally relevant, preachers across the nation are encouraging their congregations to have relations—a lot. I think they even wrote a country music song about the phenomenon: "Christian Boys and Girls Getting Down in the Pew."

Take, for example, the congregation at Fellowship Church in Grapevine, Texas. Their pastor, Ed Young Jr., challenged his married church members to engage in sexual relations for seven consecutive days. The church has some twenty thousand members—many of whom decided to take up his challenge and do the Lord's work.

"God says sex should be between a married man and a woman," Young told the Associated Press. "I think it's one of the greatest things you can do for your kids because as goes the marriage, so goes the family."[1]

I'm not too sure how around-the-clock "fellowship" fits into his argument, but not many folks seem to be complaining. For good measure the pastor delivered his "Thou Shalt Have Sex" sermon from a bed.

Seven straight days of sex? Whew. You know, even the good Lord took one day off.

And then there's the story of Relevant Church in Ybor City, Florida. Paul Wirth told his congregation he was worried about the number of married couples filing for divorce. He figured the best way to reverse the trend was for them to spend more time in bed. So Pastor Wirth ordered his married congregants to have sex for thirty days in a row.

The pastor didn't explain exactly how all that tussling in the sheets would save marriages.

He did talk about how kids, jobs, and lots of other stuff can come between a husband and wife. He talked about how they need to spend more time together. I suspect after thirty days of doing what comes naturally, it's conceivable couples could be too tired to do anything else, much less call a divorce attorney.

Anyway, the church Web site said people aren't having enough sex, and it could lead to marital problems—hence the Thirty-Day Sex Challenge. They even launched a blog to help churchgoers overcome their concerns and write about their journey. So church members were pretty pumped up, although some wondered if they would be able to muster the strength needed to fulfill their spousal obligations. It's too bad the makers of Red Bull didn't sign up as a corporate sponsor.

The single members of Relevant Church had an assignment too. They were encouraged to *refrain* from sex for thirty days. I ran the numbers and determined this would result in an equal amount of both frustrated and exhausted congregants.

I remember being in a service once where the pastor was extolling the virtues of marriage. "Brothers and sisters, I stand here today and tell you that sex is amazing! It's fantastic! It's the most incredible creation on God's green Earth!"

The obligatory "amens" and "praise the Lords" popped up around the sanctuary, and at one point the young marrieds section of the church gave him a standing ovation.

"But," the pastor chastised the crowd, "sex is only good within the boundaries set up by the Lord."

That's all well and good, but I wonder if the pastor really made his point, especially to the throngs of teenage boys in attendance. Judging from their reaction to his sex declaration, their brains shut off just after he said "sex is amazing."

If I may take a moment of personal privilege, I'd like to send a message to preachers who seem determined to preach about the greatness of intercourse. On behalf of all the Christian singles in your congregation, we get it. We understand sex is great, but we don't need to be reminded of it every Sunday. It's like the leader of Weight Watchers showing up to class with a Double Whopper. We get it.

I need to be honest, folks. I'm not all that comfortable with preachers delivering such frank talks on sex. I'm a Southern Baptist; we don't even hold hands during "Kum Ba Yah." We're more likely to speak in tongues than kiss in tongues. I was a freshman in college before I realized babies were not the product of spontaneous combustion.

All this talk about sex reminds me of an incident that occurred in the summer of 1982. I was in junior high school, and a group of us were attending our church youth camp somewhere in the wilds of Louisiana.

It was late at night, and as most junior high boys are prone to do, we were looking for trouble. But as luck would have it, trouble found us—inside a run-down, clapboard cabin at a Baptist campground. One of the guys pulled out a book wrapped in brown paper. We were half intrigued, half scared to death.

"You won't believe what I found," he said. Judging from the brown paper wrapper, I knew it couldn't have been spiritually edifying.

"It's another book of the Bible."

We all lurched away from it—afraid we might get hit by a bolt of lightning. Since childhood, I had known there were sixty-six books in the Bible, but for some reason, we only studied sixty-five.

My friend's revelation was stunning. We slowly gathered around the book. Someone flicked on a flashlight, and my friend began unwrapping the paper.

"It's called . . ." he said, "The Song of Solomon. And you won't believe what it says."

We exchanged curious looks as he started reading from the ancient texts, and it didn't take us long to figure out those mountains of myrrh and hills of frankincense weren't geological anomalies. By the time he got to the part about gazelles and sheep, Bobby Donald's voice changed.

About that time our camp counselor came walking up the steps, and we flicked off the light.

"What's going on in there?" he hollered.

"Nothing, sir. We're just reading the Bible."

"Really? Well, praise the Lord, boys! It's important to gird your loins with the gospel!"

Praise the Lord, indeed.

And that brings us back to Relevant Church in Ybor City, Florida. I'm not all that keen on uttering prophecies, but I'm willing to predict the building committee might want to start drawing up plans for a larger church nursery. They may need one in about nine months.

33

The Worship Wars

A battle is being waged in the choir lofts of America's churches. Troops adorned in flowing robes are mounting a vocal assault on contemporary praise and worship music armed with only a pitch pipe and the revered *Baptist Hymnal.*

It's being billed as this century's "worship war," and it usually involves a frazzled minister of music trying to please those who enjoy traditional hymns as well as those who do not. I'm not too sure who coined the phrase, but it sadly represents both sides in this ongoing struggle of man versus organ.

In my best guess, it comes down to a fairly simple question: Should our Sunday morning worship experience be filled with great songs of the faith, or should we orchestrate elaborate stage shows that employ musicians who use Backstreet Boy theatrics to bring honor to God? Or is it possible to have both?

I'm not sure where I stand on the issue of worship style. As a generation Xer, I feel a certain urge to slap a guitar riff or drum solo in the middle of "Holy, Holy, Holy." But as a lifelong Southern Baptist, my heart also finds comfort in the traditional songs of my childhood, songs like "Amazing Grace," "What a Friend We Have in Jesus," and "It is Well with My Soul."

Yet modern worship songs, unlike some hymns, are filled with passionate lyrics that breathe reality into church services. Like the lyrics to "You Are My King":

I'm forgiven because you were forsaken,
I'm accepted, you were condemned,
I'm alive and well,
Your spirit is within me
Because you died and rose again.[1]

Hymns don't always engender that kind of clarity. I never understood what "sheaves" were, for example, or where I was supposed to be "bringing" them. I only knew that I should "come rejoicing" wherever they were brought.

There's also not that much spontaneity with traditional worship. The service starts with an organ prelude, followed by the call to worship, the deacon's prayer, a welcome by the preacher, a few hymns, the offertory prayer, and then that moment of a lifetime for choir members—the offertory solo. Services like these are now headed the way of the dinosaur in this new church age of television lighting, pulsating video shows, professionally choreographed worship teams, and other high-tech gadgetry.

But honestly some days I truly miss those moments when the soloist would clear her throat, asking us to intercede on her behalf. You just knew your ears were in for three minutes of joyful noise—emphasis on the noise. Yet no matter how awful the singing was, you somehow knew she was wailing from the top of her lungs and the bottom of her heart.

There's still something special in that.

I believe the true victims in this battle over worship styles aren't the ones in the choir loft or behind a set of drums. They're the ones in our homes—our children.

A few summers ago I was at a church camp and came across a group of folks sitting in rocking chairs heartily singing some of the great hymns of the faith.

In my heart there rings a melody, there rings a melody of love!

A few teenagers passing by stopped, listened, and marveled at the lyrics.

"Is that a new chorus?" one of the kids asked. "I've never heard it before."

Could it be? Have we produced a generation of believers who've never heard the hymns that have sustained our forefathers through sorrow and heartache, through happiness and joy?

Maybe not.

Last week young Cousin Billy informed me that he and his college roommate, along with two girls, were going to sing in church. They formed an impromptu quartet. I wondered if they would be performing a contemporary Christian song and was genuinely surprised when Billy shook his head.

No, they chose to sing, "How Great Thou Art."

"Why that song?" I asked.

"I'm not exactly sure what I like about that song," Billy told me over cheesesteak sandwiches in Philadelphia. "It just strikes a chord in my heart. I like how it describes various scenes of nature and how great God is for creating it."

> Then sings my soul, my Savior God to Thee.
> How great Thou art, How great Thou art.
> Then sings my soul, my Savior God to Thee
> How great Thou art, How great Thou art.[2]

But for Billy the true gem of the song lay in the final verse. "It's the one about Christ's coming and the joy that will fill my heart," he said. "That's what makes it a really beautiful hymn."

> When Christ shall come, with shouts of acclamation
> And take me home, what joy shall fill my heart!
> Then I shall bow in humble adoration
> And there proclaim, "My God, how great Thou art!"[3]

So with both sides laying claim to the title of my-way-of-worship-is-better, what's a back-row Baptist to do? For starters, we could have a little give-and-take. To be honest, trying something new in the worship service every now and then sure couldn't hurt. Even "Jesus Loves Me" started out as a contemporary tune.

Maybe, just maybe, God is more interested in *why* we worship than *how* we worship.

As for those of you who still desire a worship service on the cutting edge, check out this Christian tune:

> So I'll cherish the old, rugged cross,
> 'Til my trophies at last I lay down;
> I will cling to the old rugged cross,
> And exchange it some day for a crown.[4]

You want cutting edge? Now, that's cutting edge.

34

A Christmas Eve Miracle

 It was a husband and father's worst nightmare. Mike Hermanstorfer's wife went into labor on Christmas Eve. As Tracy Hermanstorfer prepared to give birth, Mike held her hand, and without warning the unthinkable happened. Tracy went into cardiac arrest. She stopped breathing. Her heart stopped beating. Tracy Hermanstorfer was gone.

A team of doctors at Memorial Hospital in Colorado Springs furiously worked to save the unborn child, but the baby was delivered lifeless with barely a hint of a heartbeat.

In a matter of moments, Mike's Christmas Eve was filled with sorrow. His wife and newborn son were gone. Doctors were eventually able to revive the little boy, but his mother—not even so much as a pulse.

Then something strange happened—something that to this day puzzles the medical experts. Nearly four minutes after her heart stopped beating, she came back to life.

"We did a thorough evaluation and can't find anything that explains why this happened,"[1] Dr. Stephanie Martin told the Associated Press.

But Mike and Tracy believe they know exactly what happened. It was "the hand of God," Mike told reporters. "We are both believers, but this right here, even a nonbeliever—you explain to me how this happened. There is no other explanation."

The doctor said she wasn't sure if she had help from on high but acknowledged, "Wherever I can get the help, I'll take it."

The story of the Hermanstorfers reminds me of a survey published in the journal *Sociology of Religion*. It indicates that most Americans believe God is involved in their everyday lives.[2] The survey also reveals Americans believe God is concerned with their personal well-being. An impressive 82 percent said they depend on God for help and guidance in making decisions.

Even more interesting, to me, is this one little nugget: 71 percent believe when things happen, good or bad, it's part of the Lord's plan for their lives.

Interestingly enough the survey reports people who make more money or have more degrees behind their names are less likely to believe in divine intervention. In other words, the smarter you are, the dumber you become.

I'm sure the experts will try to find some sort of scientific explanation for what happened to the Hermanstorfers, and there will certainly be naysayers who refute any sort of divine intervention on that Christmas Eve in Colorado Springs. But I'm not too sure the Hermanstorfers will be swayed.

One of my favorite George Strait songs, "I Saw God Today," addresses this very issue.

> I've been to church,
> I've read the book.
> I know He's there,
> But I don't look
> Near as often as I should.
> His fingerprints are everywhere
> I just slow down to stop and stare,
> Open my eyes and, man, I swear,
> I saw God today.[3]

And then I think about the Hermanstorfer family. I think about the day God saw fit to bless them with a miracle. And in the years to come, as they watch their little boy grow into a man, one day they will tell him about a miraculous birth on a Christmas Eve—not in Bethlehem but in Colorado Springs, Colorado. The night a husband and wife saw the hand of God.

It's the End of the World as We Know It

 President Obama believes people who cling to their guns and religion are bitter Americans. Maybe the reason we cling to our guns and religion is because we're afraid he might take them away. And for that matter, it's not so much that we are bitter Americans. I just think we have a bad case of indigestion.

The mainstream media and the ruling class treat us like children. They preach the gospel of civility but mock us with disdain and condescension.

"They're too stupid," said HBO host Bill Maher on TBS. "They're like a dog."

John Hickelooper, the Democratic mayor of Denver, called us "backward thinkers."

Actress Janeane Garofalo called the Tea Party racist, saying, "This is racism straight up and is nothing but a bunch of teabagging rednecks."

Attorney General Eric Holder called us a "nation of cowards."

First Lady Michelle Obama said, in noting the kind of changes that backlight and support much of what I've discussed in this book, "For the first time in my adult life, I am proud of my country."

Perhaps one of the most telling examples of this hatred toward our nation came from an Obama nominee to the federal court, Judge Edward Chen. The following paragraphs appeared in *The Washington Times* in 2009.

> Judge Chen's words speak for themselves. When the congregation sang "America the Beautiful" at a funeral, Judge Chen told the audience of his "feelings of ambivalence and cynicism when confronted with appeals to patriotism—sometimes I cannot help but feel that there are too much [sic] injustice and too many inequalities that prevent far too many Americans from enjoying the beauty extolled in that anthem."
>
> In a speech on Sept. 22, 2001, he said that among his first responses to the Sept. 11 terrorist attacks on America was a "sickening feeling in my stomach about what might happen to race relations and religious tolerance on our own soil. . . . One has to wonder whether the seemingly irresistible forces of racism, nativism and scapegoating which has [sic] recurred so often in our history can be effectively restrained."[1]

Funny, when I hear people sing "America the Beautiful," I have feelings of gratitude and thanksgiving that God would shed His grace on a people so undeserving.

Paula Deen knows about that grace. One of the most wonderfully kind and generous chefs in the nation had a difficult lot in life. "I didn't have two nickels to rub together," she told me. "So it makes me very appreciative and very grateful for everything."

Miss Paula is proof that anyone can achieve the American dream. "I have worked hard. But God, in turn, has blessed that hard work. And it's important when we're blessed that we pay it forward and try to help someone else."

It's that type of spirit that built a nation—a nation of free men and women who trusted God and not the government. If you believe liberal lawmakers and the mainstream media, we are a nation who no longer believes in God. But that's just not true.

Congressman Randy Forbes, a Republican from the Commonwealth of Virginia and chairman of the Congressional Prayer Caucus, addressed this issue in *U.S. News & World Report.*

> So, if America was birthed upon Judeo-Christian principles, at what point in time did our nation cease to be Judeo-Christian? It was not when a small minority tried to remove the name of God from our public buildings and monuments. It was not when they tried to remove God from our veterans' flag-folding ceremonies or to take the motto off our coins. Nor was it when this small minority fought to banish prayer from our schools, strip the 10 Commandments from our courtrooms or remove the phrase "one nation under God" from the new Capitol Visitor Center.
>
> No, the answer is clear: While America has always welcomed individuals of diverse faiths and non-faith, we have never ceased to be a Judeo-Christian nation. That small minority could tear references of faith off every building and document across our nation, but it would not change the fact that we were built on Judeo-Christian principles.[2]

According to Gallup, 78 percent of Americans consider themselves Christian. So what does that tell us?

It tells us President Obama was off the mark when he told the Christian Broadcasting Network in 2007 that the United States was "no longer just a Christian nation." On the contrary, Mr. President, I say again—the United States is overwhelmingly a Christian nation.

Friends, I hope you know that Christ alone is the author of our freedom. Without Him, without His guiding hand, our nation will cease being free.

Throughout my travels across this great nation, I've discovered some wonderful people—my fellow countrymen. I've met police officers and firefighters, nurses and school teachers. I've met soldiers and veterans, Boy Scouts and Girl Scouts. I've met pastors and journalists, farmers and construction workers.

I've watched them pledge allegiance to the flag, to one nation under God. I've heard their stories of defending our nation from the halls of Montezuma to the shores of Tripoli. They go to work. They go to church. They go hunting and fishing. They go to Little League games and Sunday dinners on the grounds.

I've watched the sun rise over Egg Harbor Township in New Jersey and watched the sun set over the Golden Gate Bridge in San Francisco. I've taken a riverboat ride on the mighty Mississippi and climbed the Great Smoky Mountains.

I've had barbecue in Memphis and gumbo in New Orleans, deep-dish pizza in Chicago and a hot dog from a street cart in New York City. I've dined on Moon Pies in Chattanooga and Sonora Dogs in Tucson.

I've watched a stickball game in Brooklyn and a baseball game in Atlanta. I've run the New York City Marathon and welcomed in the new year in Times Square.

This is the America I know. This is the America I love.

But our nation and our world is at a precarious point in history. Many folks, Christian and non-Christian, are asking the same question: What is this world coming to?

According to the Bible, this world is coming to an end. For generations we've heard the prophecies—earthquakes, fires, floods, famine, wars. There is turmoil and unrest in the land. There is sadness and sorrow. A sense of hopelessness seems to grip the country. But, friends, as I write these words, I do so from a heart filled with joy. That's because this world is not my home. And if you are a believer in Jesus Christ, it's not your home either. We're just passing through.

The Bible calls us aliens in this world. Aliens are people who have placed their hope and trust in Jesus Christ. There's a song made famous by R.E.M. called "It's the End of the World as We Know It."[3] There's a bit of truth in that tune. It is the end of the world as we know it. And you know something? I feel just fine.

When I was a little boy growing up in the South, I walked down the aisle of a Southern Baptist church and accepted Jesus Christ as my Lord and Savior. Romans 10:13 tells us, "Everyone who calls upon the name of the Lord will be saved."

And one day, perhaps soon, Jesus is going to return to take His people home. One of my favorite gospel songs talks about a "Great Gettin' Up Morning." And on that glorious day, I don't know about you, but I plan on getting up and going somewhere special.

36

The End

 Wolf Blitzed: This is breaking news on the Global News Network. Strange events are happening across the country both in the sky and on the ground. New York City's 911 system was overwhelmed just moments ago by complaints of loud horn sections blasting across the boroughs. We tried to reach city officials but were unable to hear their responses because of what sounded like trumpets sounding in the distance. Civil defense sirens have sounded in most American cities, and people are being urged to take shelter immediately. Live on the phone with us is General John Bigguns from NORAD. Sir, what can you tell us?

General Bigguns: Wolf, we've never seen anything like it. Our radar systems are overwhelmed right now. We're tracking hundreds, if not thousands of targets.

Wolf Blitzed: Dear Lord! Are we all doomed? Which cities will be hit first?

General Bigguns: Uh, I think you might have misunderstood, Wolf. These aren't incoming targets.

Wolf Blitzed: I'm confused, General.

General Bigguns: Wolf, these are outbound targets.

Wolf Blitzed: We'll get back to the general in just a few moments, but right now I want to bring in Dr. Rashad Guppie,

GNN's chief environmental reporter. According to eyewitness accounts the clouds are rolling back, and it appears the sky is opening. Got any answers for us?

Dr. Guppie: Wolf, it's pretty obvious what is happening. Former Vice President Al Gore has just released a statement, and he believes the parting of the clouds is a direct result of climate change. Mr. Gore said it's imperative Americans immediately reduce their carbon imprint.

Wolf Blitzed: Certainly makes sense to me, Dr. Guppie. In the meantime let's go live to Washington, DC, where our sexy blonde reporter is standing by.

Sexy Blonde Reporter: Wolf, I'm at the Tomb of the Unknowns, and I've gotta tell you, my surgically enhanced body is shivering all over. Just moments ago the ground started shaking, and the grave markers began falling over.

Wolf Blitzed: An earthquake, Sexy Blonde Reporter?

Sexy Blonde Reporter: That's what I thought at first, Wolf. But then the lids on the coffins started opening up and . . .

Wolf Blitzed: Tell us, Sexy Blonde Reporter, tell us what you see.

Sexy Blonde Reporter: Wolf, I see dead people, and I think they're alive.

Wolf Blitzed: I don't mean to interrupt you, but we're now getting reports of breaking news onboard the Space Shuttle *Endeavor*. Let's listen in to this live feed from the Johnson Space Center in Houston.

Endeavor: Uh Houston, we've got a problem.

Houston: All systems appear to be functioning normally, *Endeavor*.

Endeavor: It's not mechanical, Houston. We're picking up some unidentified flying objects.

Houston: Could you repeat that, *Endeavor*. Your last transmission was a bit garbled. Sounded like you said some UFOs were flying around up there.

Endeavor: Affirmative, Houston. Unidentified flying objects, and there are a lot of them.

Houston: You boys drinking something up there?

Endeavor: That's a negative, Houston. The objects appear to be human in nature and seem to be fairly docile. We've observed many of them smiling—sweet mercy, Houston!

Houston: What is it, *Endeavor?* What's going on up there?

Endeavor: I could've sworn I just saw Jerry Falwell floating by the shuttle bay. He was holding a sign.

Houston: A sign? What did it say?

Endeavor: "I told you so."

Wolf Blitzed: Obviously something delusional is happening onboard the shuttle. We will keep you posted. We're also monitoring developments overseas in Europe. Correspondent Jacques LePew is live in Paris. Jacques?

Jacques: Bonjour, Wolf. Seems like a normal day in gay Paris! Nothing out of zee ordinary to report.

Wolf Blitzed: Thanks, Jacques. We're getting similar reports from London, Moscow, and most of western Europe. We've also tried reaching out to some of the nation's religious leaders, but so far no one has returned our calls. Wait just a moment—I'm being told the president is about to address the nation. Let's go live to the White House.

POTUS: My fellow Americans, we are witnessing extraordinary events across the nation. There are reports of citizens simply vanishing into thin air, of four massive creatures on horses galloping across the plains of Texas. It's unclear what is behind these disappearances, but you can rest easy knowing that the top minds in my government are on top of this. My team is fired up and ready to go. So far, most of the disappearances have occurred in the South and Midwest. Most of our major cities— Los Angeles, San Francisco, Seattle, and New York—appear to be largely unscathed. At this point I believe it is prudent to stay home, listen to the instructions of your local authorities, and find solace with a politically correct, government-sanctioned deity. Thank you and may the aforementioned politically correct, government-sanctioned deity bless America.

Wolf Blitzed: I believe we now have a reporter set to go live from Times Square. Do we have the shot? Excellent. Let's go live to Times Square and reporter Todd Starnes.

Wolf Blitzed: Todd?

Wolf Blitzed: Todd?

Wolf Blitzed: Todd?

Notes

Introduction

1. Mayhill Fowler, "Obama: No Surprise That Hard-Pressed Pennsylvanians Turn Bitter," *The Huffington Post*, (April 11, 2008), http://www.huffingtonpost.com/mayhill-fowler/obama-no-surprise-that-ha_b_96188.html.
2. Toby Keith, "Courtesy of the Red, White, and Blue," Dreamworks Nashville, 2001.
3. Quote from *Gone with the Wind*, Selznick International Pictures, Warner Brothers, 1939.
4. Alexander Slidell Mackenzie, *Life of Stephen Decatur: A Commodore in the Navy of the United States* (Boston, MA: 1846), 295.
5. Lee Greenwood "Proud to Be An American", MCA, Nashville, 1984.

Chapter 1

1. Michael Lind, "America Is not a Christian Nation" (April 14, 2009), Dispatches from DC, http://www.salon.com/news/opinion/feature/2009/04/14/christian_nation.

Chapter 4

1. Jim Garamone, "Officials Reject Allegations of Proselytizing in Afghanistan" (May 5, 2009) http://www.af.mil/news/story.asp?id-123147725.
2. Ashish Kumar Sen, "Koran Protest Stokes Emotions," *The Washington Times* (September 7, 2010), http://www.washingtontimes.com/news/2010/sep/7/petraeus-koran-burning-could-endanger-troops.
3. Matthew Lee, "Clinton, Gates Denounce Planned Koran Burning," *The Washington Times* (September 8, 2010), http://www.washingtontimes.com/news/2010/sep/8/clinton-gates-denounce-planned-koran-burning.
4. Chad Groening, "Holy Book Burnings Spark Hypocrisy," One News Now (September 9, 2010), http://www.onenewsnow.com/Culture/Default.aspx?id=1160612.

Chapter 5

1. Andrea Stone, "Congress Urged to Drop Evangelist from Event," AOL News (April 26, 2010), http://www.aolnews.com/2010/04/26/muslim-group-wants-graham-booted-from-prayer-event.

Chapter 7

1. Sasha Johnson and Candy Crowley, "Winfrey Tells Iowa Crowd: Barack Obama Is 'the One," CNNPolitics

(December 8, 2007), http://articles.cnn.com/2007-12-08/politics/oprah.
obama_1_gayle-king-barack-obama-oprah-winfrey?_s=PM:POLITICS.

2. Geoff Mulvihill Scrutiny rises over NJ kids singing Obama song,
Burlington County Times (September 25, 2009), http://www.breitbart.com/
article.php?id=D9AUGK080&show_article=1.

3. Kyle Hill Bryan Glover, "When You're Holding a Hammer, Everything
Looks like a Nail," (2010).

Chapter 9

1. "Snowpocalypse to Snowicane: Hype Reigns," Associated Press
(February 28, 2010), http://www.msnbc.msn.com/id/35627330/ns/weather/t/
snowpocalypse-snowicane-hype-reigns.

2. "Energy Crisis Threatens U.S. Survival, Gore Says," Associated
Press (July 17, 2008), http://articles.cnn.com/2008-07-17/politics/gore.
energy_1_read-gore-carbon-free-carbon-dioxide?_s=PM:POLITICS.

3. Albert Gore, *An Inconvenient Truth: the Planetary Emergency of Global
Warming and What We Can Do about It* (New York: Rodale, 2006).

Chapter 10

1. Sheryl Gay Stolberg, "The Spotlight's Bright Glare", *The New York Times*
(December 4, 2009), http://www.nytimes.com/2009/12/06/fashion/06desiree.
html.

2. See http://www.foxnews.com/opinion/2009/12/07/
eric-metaxas-white-house-creche-jesus-christmas.

3. "Simon Doonan," *The New York Times* (January 10, 2011), http://top-
ics.nytimes.com/top/reference/timestopics/people/d/simon_doonan/index.
html?s=oldest&.

4. Colby Hall, "Andrew Breitbart and WH Designer Simon Doonan Spar
Over 'Tinselgate,'" Mediaite (January 6, 2010), http://www.mediaite.com/
online/andrew-breitbart-and-white-house-designer-simon-doonan-spar-over-
ornamentgate.

Chapter 12

1. Todd Starnes, "Cop Orders Kids to Stop Praying at Supreme Court,"
FOX News (July 15, 2010), http://www.foxnews.com/us/2010/07/15/
students-ordered-stop-praying-outside-supreme-court-building.

Chapter 14

1. "TIME Poll Results: Americans' Views on the Campaign, Religion and
the Mosque Controversy," *TIME* magazine (August 18, 2010), http://www.time.
com/time/politics/article/0,8599,2011680-1,00.html.

2. "Growing Number of Americans Say Obama Is a Muslim," Pew Research
Center Publications (August 19, 2010), http://pewresearch.org/pubs/1701/
poll-obama-muslim-christian-church-out-of-politics-political-leaders-religious.

3. Barack Obama, *The Audacity of Hope: Thoughts on Reclaiming the
American Dream* (New York: Crown, 2006).

4. Brian Ross, "Obama's Pastor: God Damn America, U.S. to Blame for

9/11," ABC News via *The New York Time* (March 13, 2008), http://abcnews.
go.com/Blotter/DemocraticDebate/story?id=4443788&page=1.

5. Nicholas D. Kristof, "The Push to 'Otherize' Obama," *The New York Times* (September 20, 2008), http://www.nytimes.com/2008/09/21/opinion/21kristof.html.

6. "Obama Drops 'Creator' from Declaration quote," WorldNetDaily (September 18, 2010), http://www.wnd.com/?pageId=204973.

7. "Obama Administration Opposes FDR Prayer at WWII Memorial," FOX News (November 4, 2011), http://www.foxnews.com/politics/2011/11/04/obama-administration-opposes-fdr-prayer-at-wwii-memorial.

8. Nicholas Ballasy Edwin Mora, "After Covering Up Symbol for Jesus at Georgetown, White House Had Obama Speak in Front of Symbols for AMA, AARP, and Human Rights Campaign," CNS News (December 16, 2009), http://www.cnsnews.com/news/article/58661.

Chapter 15

1. Rita Savard, "Parents: Chelmsford School Holding Firm on Holiday Gift-shop Restrictions," *Lowell Sun*, (November 14, 2009).

2. Jennifer Riley, "Parents Take Action Against Christmas Restrictions in Schools," *The Christian Post* (December 10, 2009), http://www.christianpost.com/news/parents-take-action-against-christmas-restrictions-in-schools-42226.

3. Todd Starnes, "Second Graders Sing About Allah?" FOX News via *The Indianapolis Star* (December 14, 2009), http://radio.foxnews.com/2009/12/14/public-school-kids-singing-to-allah.

4. Ibid.

5. Ibid.

6. Gareth McGrath and Chelsea Kellner, "School Board Reinstates Rudolph, Santa," *Wilmington Star News Online* (December 5, 2008), http://www.starnewsonline.com/article/20081205/ARTICLES/812050251.

7. Kendall Hatch, "Holliston Firefighters Angry at Town for Banning Cross Atop Fire Station," *The Metrowest Daily News* (December 10, 2009), http://www.metrowestdailynews.com/state/x1582019835/Holliston-firefighters-angry-at-town-for-banning-cross-atop-fire-station.

8. Eric Ferreri, "UNC Libraries to Forgo Christmas Trees," *The Charlotte Observer* (December 5, 2008).

9. Jesse McKinley, "After Complaint about a Star, an Order to Remove Religious Symbols," *The New York Times* (December 22, 2009), http://www.nytimes.com/2009/12/23/us/23tree.html?adxnnl=1&adxnnlx=1305576082-WoV/+2z8FCCelfVFthyS/g.

10. Todd Starnes, "University Silences Christmas Bells," FOX News Radio (December 20, 2010), http://radio.foxnews.com/2010/12/10/university-silences-christmas-bells.

11. Carly O'Keefe, "Christmas Carols Silenced in SIU Bell Tower," KFVS-TV 12 News (December 9, 2010), http://www.kfvs12.com/story/13648674/christmas-carols-silenced-in-siu-belltower?redirected=true.

12. "SIU Clock Stops Chiming Christmas Music," WSIL-TV (December 9, 2010), http://www.wsiltv.com/p/news_details.php?newsID=11837&type=top.

Chapter 16

1. Kix Brooks and Ronnie Dunn, "That's What It's All About," Arista, Nashville (2004).

Chapter 17

1. Jeff. Poor, "We Believe That One Day the Flag of Islam Will Fly Over the White House," News Busters (October 3, 2010), http://newsbusters.org/blogs/jeff-poor/2010/10/03/week-wages-holy-war-month-midterms-we-believe-one-day-flag-islam-will-fly.

2. Charlie Butts, "Ex-coach Sues School District over Religion," Associated Press via One News Now (July 28, 2009), http://www.onenewsnow.com/Legal/Default.aspx?id=621726.

3. "Four Christian Evangelists Arrested at Arab festival," the Associated Press via Mlive.com (June 20, 2010), http://www.mlive.com/news/detroit/index.ssf/2010/06/four_christian_evangelists_arr.html.

4. Laura Clark, "Parents in Uproar over School Meals for Muslims," *Daily Mail* (February 09, 2007), http://www.dailymail.co.uk/news/article-435277/Parents-uproar-school-meals-Muslims.html.

5. Colin Fernandez and Nick McDermott, "Public Pool Bars Father and Son from its 'Muslim-only' Swimming Session," *Daily Mail* (April 18, 2008), http://www.dailymail.co.uk/news/article-560231/Public-pool-bars-father-son-Muslim-swimming-session.html.

6. Yoav Gonen "HS Test 'Slams' Christianity, Lauds Islam," *New York Post* (August 24, 2010), http://www.nypost.com/p/news/local/bad_faith_in_regents_exam_IHsTi7lMbqhfdMDrnF3xYL.

7. Todd Starnes and Patrick Manning, "Oklahoma Police Captain Faces Disciplinary Action for Refusing to Attend Islamic Event," FOX News (February 23, 2011), http://www.foxnews.com/us/2011/02/23/oklahoma-police-captain-refuses-attend-islamic-event.

Chapter 18

1. Phillip Matier and Andrew Ross, "Possible A's Sites a Case of Fantasy Baseball?" *San Francisco Chronicle* (November 30, 2009), http://articles.sfgate.com/2009-11-30,/bay-area/17181498_1_howard-street-lew-wolff-sites.

2. "Idea of Public Sex Tents is Way out of Line," *San Francisco Chronicle* (December 2, 2009), http://www.sfgate.com/cgi-bin/article.cgi?f=/c/a/2009/12/02/ED1Q1AT98G.DTL.

3. John Coté, "Sugary-drink Ban Starts to Affect S.F. Sites," *San Francisco Chronicle* (July 06, 2010), http://articles.sfgate.com/2010-07-06/bay-area/21939137_1_vending-machines-soda-obesity.

4. Carolyn Jones, "S.F. Considers Banning Sale of Pets Except Fish," *San Francisco Chronicle* (July 08, 2010), http://articles.sfgate.com/2010-07-08/news/21941947_1_animal-control-pet-store-hamsters.

Chapter 19

1. Brian Hughes, "Crestview Cub Scout Saves Grandmother's Life," Crestview News Bulletin (March 9, 2011), http://www.crestviewbulletin.com/articles/cub-13500-grandmother-scout.html.

2. Chad Tucker, "Greensboro Boy Finds and Returns Purse with $2,000 Inside," FOX WGHP-TV (December 16, 2009), http://www.myfox8.com/news/wghp-boy-finds-purse-091216,0,440194.story.

3. Anthony York, "Assembly Kills Resolution Honoring Boy Scouts," Los Angeles Times (April 13, 2010), http://latimesblogs.latimes.com/california-politics/2010/04/assembly-kills-resolution-honoring-boy-scouts.html.

4. "Military Bases Are Told Not to Sponsor Boy Scout Troops," Associated Press via The Washington Post (November 16, 2004), http://www.washington-post.com/wp-dyn/articles/A52547-2004Nov15.html.

5. Ibid.

6. See http://www.ru12.org/2010/03/ru12-executive-director-comments-about-vt-funding-for-the-boy-scouts.html.

7. Ibid.

8. Jarrett. Renshaw "Union Troubled by Scout Project," The Morning Call (November 15, 2009), http://articles.mcall.com/2009-11-15/news/4476519_1_eagle-scout-nick-balzano-seiu-members.

Chapter 20

1. Mark Simpson, "Here Come the Mirror Men," The Independent (November 15, 1994).

2. Alan Jay Lerner (lyrics), Frederick Loewe (music), "Why Can't a Woman Be More like a Man," My Fair Lady, (1961).

3. Simon Dumenco, "Should a Man Show Nipple?" Details (July 2005), http://www.details.com/style-advice/rules-of-style/200507/why-men-should-not-show-nipple-under-tight-shirts.

4. "Should Men Wear Makeup?" AskMen.com (2008), http://www.ask-men.com/daily/austin_60/95b_fashion_style.html.

5. "Discuss: Should NYC Men Dress like Women?" Page Six Magazine (September 7, 2008), http://www.nypost.com/pagesixmag/issues/20080907/Discuss+Should+NYC+Men+Dress+Women.

6. Bob Allen, "Prof Says Boys Raised to Be 'Too Soft' Will Be Ineffective Men," Associated Baptist Press (August 23, 2010), http://www.abpnews.com/content/view/5465/53.

Chapter 21

1. Barbara Kantrowitz and Pat Wingert, "Are We Facing a Gender-less Future?" Newsweek, (August 16, 2010) ,http://www.newsweek.com/2010/08/16/life-without-gender.html.

2. Todd Starnes, "'Mother,' 'Father' Changing to 'Parent One,' 'Parent Two' on Passport Applications," FOX News (January 7, 2011), http://www.foxnews.com/politics/2011/01/07/passport-applications-soon-gender-neutral.

3. Alec MacGillis, "Obama's Father's Day Proclamation, with a Nod to the Nontraditional," *The Washington Post* (June 20, 2010) http://voices.washingtonpost.com/44/2010/06/obamas-father-day-proclamation.html?wprss=44

4. Michael Jones, "President Obama's Father's Day Nod to Gay Dads," Change.org (June 20, 2010), http://news.change.org/stories/president-obamas-fathers-day-nod-to-gay-dads.

5. "Evolution of a N.J. Cross-Dressing Controversy," Associated Press via MSNBC News (April 14, 2010), http://www.msnbc.msn.com/id/36520384/ns/us_news-life.

6. Michael Carl, "'Biology-based' Restrooms Called 'Discrimination,'" WorldNetDaily (March 1, 2010), http://www.wnd.com/index.php?fa=PAGE.view&pageId=126662.

7. Kevin Miller, "HRC Panel Postpones Transgender Guidelines," *Bangor Daily News* (April 13, 2010), http://new.bangordailynews.com/2010/04/13/politics/hrc-panel-postpones-transgender-guidelines.

8. Bradley Olson, "Parker Extends City Rights Policy to Transgendered," *Houston Chronicle* (April 3, 2010), http://www.chron.com/disp/story.mpl/metropolitan/6941909.html.

9. Lawrence D. Jones, "Houston Clergy at Arms over Lesbian Mayor's Orders," *The Christian Post* (April 6, 2010), http://www.christianpost.com/news/houston-clergy-at-arms-over-lesbian-mayors-orders-44637.

Chapter 22

1. "Florida Man Loses Arm to Alligator During Attack," Associated Press via FOX News Channel (November 29, 2006), http://www.foxnews.com/story/0%2C2933%2C232821%2C00.html.

2. Damien Cave, "Intentions of Whale Killing Are Debated," *The New York Times* (February 25, 2010), http://www.nytimes.com/2010/02/26/us/26whale.html.

3. Cass R. Sunstein, "The Rights of Animals: A Very Short Primer" (August 2002), University Chicago Law & Economics, Olin Working Paper No. 157, University of Chicago, Public Law Research Paper No. 30.

Chapter 24

1. Stephanie Innes, "No-Oreo Zone: Kids at School Can't Bring Processed Food," *Arizona Daily Star* (April 14, 2010), http://www.azcentral.com/news/articles/2010/04/14/20100414arizona-school-bans-processed-food-for-kids.html.

2. "Boy Banned from Eating Cheese Sandwich," *The Telegraph* (April 28, 2010), http://www.telegraph.co.uk/education/educationnews/7643996/Boy-banned-from-eating-cheese-sandwich.html.

3. Claire Aasen, "'Meatless Monday' Continues to Spur Student Controversy," *The Bowdoin Orient* (February 25, 2011), http://orient.bowdoin.edu/orient/article.php?date=2011-02-25&section=1&id=4.

4. Sam Petulla, "No Meat for You!" *Inside Higher Ed* (March 1, 2011), http://www.insidehighered.com/news/2011/03/01/bowdoin_faces_backlash_over_day_without_meat_in_dining_halls.

5. Gabe Gutierrez, "Jolly Rancher Lands Brazos ISD Third-Grader in

Detention for a Week," KHOU-TV (May 6, 2010), http://www.khou.com/news/Candy-Gets-Third-Grader-A-Weeks-Detention-93033319.html.

6. Tom Yerace, "Kids Hunger for More School Lunch at Highlands," *Valley News Dispatch* (September 17, 2010), mhttp://www.pittsburghlive.com/x/valleynewsdispatch/s_699979.html.

7. "Cupcakes Banned at Elementary School," WDIV-TV (September 15, 2010), http://www.clickondetroit.com/news/25024560/detail.html.

8. Monica Eng and Joel Hood, "Chicago School Bans Some Lunches Brought from Home," *Chicago Tribune* (April 11, 2011), http://articles.chicagotribune.com/2011-04-11/news/ct-met-school-lunch-restrictions-041120110410_1_lunch-food-provider-public-school.

9. Mara Gay, "Chicago School Bans Bag Lunches to Get Kids to Eat Less Junk Food," AOL News (April 11, 2011), http://www.aolnews.com/2011/04/11/chicago-school-bans-bag-lunches-to-get-kids-to-eat-less-junk-food.

10. Ikimulisa Livingston, Beth Stebner, and Leonard Greene, "Nanny Mayor: Salt Is like Asbestos," *New York Post* (January 12, 2010), http://www.nypost.com/p/news/local/with_grain_of_salt_lIknBse7gfp3PUP5hq6ZBK.

11. Jennifer Medina, "A Crackdown on Bake Sales in City Schools," *The New York Times* (October 2, 2009), http://www.nytimes.com/2009/10/03/nyregion/03bakesale.html.

12. Catherine Yang, "Councilman Gioia Proposes Fast Food Ban Near Schools," *The Epoch Times* (April 20, 2009), http://www.theepochtimes.com/n2/content/view/15668.

13. Rachel Gordon, "Plan to Limit Toys with Meals Faces 1st Test," *San Francisco Chronicle* (September 25, 2010), http://www.sfgate.com/cgi-bin/article.cgi?f=/c/a/2010/09/25/MN9A1FIIPK.DTL.

Chapter 25

1. Reuven Fenton, Ada Calhoun, and Dan Mangan, "Rutgers Freshman Commits Suicide after Roommate Puts Sex Tape Online," *New York Post* (September 30, 2010), http://www.nypost.com/p/news/local/cruelcam_costs_kid_life_gKIl4DmNjUdOJ4ZMdNy12N.

Chapter 26

1. Ryan Wilson, "William & Mary Crowns Jessee Vasold First Transgender Homecoming Queen," *The Flat Hat* via AOL News (October 26, 2009), http://www.aolnews.com/2009/10/26/william-and-mary-crowns-jessee-vasold-first-transgender-homecoming.

2. "William and Mary Students Elect Transgender Homecoming Queen," Associated Press via *The Washington Post* (October 24, 2009), http://www.washingtonpost.com/wp-dyn/content/article/2009/10/24/AR2009102401524.html?wprss=rss_metro.

3. Ari B. Bloomekatz, "Fairfax High's Prom Queen Is a Guy," *Los Angeles Times* (May 28, 2009), http://articles.latimes.com/2009/may/28/local/me-prom-queen28.

4. Annie Gowen, "Work That Tiara, Boy!" *The Washington Post*

(February 20, 2009), http://www.washingtonpost.com/wp-dyn/content/article/2009/02/19/AR2009021901780.html?hpid=sec-education.

5. Kathleen Gilbert, "George Mason Picks Homosexual Male Crossdresser for Homecoming Queen," *Catholic Exchange* (February 24th, 2009), http://catholicexchange.com/2009/02/24/116190.

Chapter 27

1. Pru Sowers, "School Leaders OK Condom Policy in Provincetown," *Provincetown Banner* (June 11, 2010), http://www.wickedlocal.com/provincetown/news/x1417293505/School-leaders-OK-condom-policy-in-Provincetown#axzz1MilOSDdl.

2. Ronnie Polaneczky, "Ronnie Polaneczky: If You Think 11-Year-Olds in This City Don't Need Condoms, Think Again," *Philadelphia Daily News* (April 13, 2011), http://articles.philly.com/2011-04-13/news/29413998_1_free-condoms-hiv-treatment-sexual-initiation.

3. Nancy Amons, "Dad Complains About Sex Class, WSMV-TV (April 09, 2010), http://www.wsmv.com/news/23108626/detail.html.

Chapter 28

1. Alec Melman, "School Says Game of Tag Is Out," FOX News (June 20, 2002), http://www.foxnews.com/story/0,2933,55836,00.html.

2. Emily Bazar, "'Not It!' More Schools Ban Games at Recess," *USA Today* (June 27, 2006), http://www.usatoday.com/news/health/2006-06-26-recess-bans_x.htm.

3. Alison Leigh Cowan "School Recess Gets Gentler, and the Adults Are Dismayed," *The New York Times* (December 14, 2007), http://www.nytimes.com/2007/12/14/education/14recess.html.

4. Rawson Marshall Thurber, *Dodgeball: A True Underdog Story*, 20th Century Fox, Red Hour Productions, (2004).

Chapter 29

1. "School Field Trip to Same-Sex Wedding Fuels Debate on Gay Marriage Ban," Associated Press via FOX News (October 22, 2008), http://www.foxnews.com/story/0,2933,443681,00.html.

2. "Equality's Winding Path," *The New York Times* (November 5, 2008), http://www.nytimes.com/2008/11/06/opinion/06thu1.html?oref=slogin.

3. "Senate Bill Seeks Teaching of Gay History," Associated Press via *The Washington Times* (April 14, 2011), http://www.washingtontimes.com/news/2011/apr/14/senate-bill-seeks-teaching-of-gay-history/.

4. "Store Refuses Gay Group's Cookie Order," WISH-TV (September 24, 2010), http://www.wishtv.com/dpp/news/local/marion_county/store-refuses-gay-groups-cookie-order.

5. Bob Unruh, "District Gags 14-Year-Olds after 'Gay' Indoctrination," WorldNetDaily (March 13, 2007), http://www.wnd.com/?pageId=40598.

6. Todd Starnes, "COURT: University Can Expel Student over Religious Beliefs," ToddStarnes.com (July 28, 2010), http://toddstarnes.com/2010/07/court-university-can-expel-student-over-religious-beliefs.

7. "Lauren Ashley, Miss Beverly Hills 2010: Bible Is 'Black and White' about Killing Homosexuals," FOX News via *Huffington Post* (February 24, 2010), http://www.huffingtonpost.com/2010/02/24/lauren-ashley-miss-beverl_n_475536.html.

8. Perez Hilton, "The City Disowns Miss Beverly Hills!" Perezhilton.com (February 24, 2010), http://perezhilton.com/2010-02-24-the-city-disowns-miss-beverly-hills.

9. Martha Groves, "'Miss Beverly Hills' Moniker Has City Crying Foul," *Los Angeles Times* (February 25, 2010), http://articles.latimes.com/2010/feb/25/local/la-me-miss-beverly-hills25-2010feb25.

10. Amy Graff, "Is San Francisco's Castro Neighborhood Appropriate for Young Kids?" *San Francisco Chronicle* (April 05, 2011), http://www.sfgate.com/cgi-bin/blogs/sfmoms/detail?entry_id=86303.

11. David Kupelian, *The Marketing of Evil: How Radicals, Elitists, and Pseudo-Experts Sell Us Corruption Disguised as Freedom* (Nashville, TN: WND, 2005).

12. Kathy Lynn Gray, "Free-Speech Fights Flare on Campuses," *The Columbus Dispatch* (April 21, 2006), http://www.dispatch.com/live/contentbe/dispatch/2006/04/21/20060421-A1-02.html.

13. "Judge Rebuffs Christian in 'Marketing of Evil' Lawsuit," WorldNetDaily (June 08, 2010), http://www.wnd.com/index.php?fa=PAGE.view&pageId=164493.

14. "British Christian Couple Lose Foster Care Rights Because They Disapprove of Homosexuality," The Associated Press via Yahoo! News (February 28, 2011), http://ca.news.yahoo.com/british-christian-couple-lose-foster-care-rights-because-20110228-103440-923.html

15. "Court Upholds Foster Ban on Couple Who Oppose Homosexuality," *Pink News* (February 28, 2011), http://www.pinknews.co.uk/2011/02/28/court-upholds-foster-ban-on-couple-who-oppose-homosexuality.

Chapter 30

1. Frank Newport, "This Christmas, 78% of Americans Identify as Christian," Gallup (December 24, 2009), http://www.gallup.com/poll/124793/this-christmas-78-americans-identify-christian.aspx.

2. Nathan Black, "Most Americans Say Judges Are Anti-Religious," *The Christian Post* (April 26, 2010), http://www.christianpost.com/news/most-americans-say-judges-are-anti-religious-44901.

3. "Minn. Legislator Wants Jesus out of Senate Prayers," Associated Press via TwinCities.com (March 16, 2011), http://www.twincities.com/national/ci_17626083?nclick_check=1.

4. Todd Starnes, "Michigan Woman Faces Civil Rights Complaint for Seeking a Christian Roommate," FOX News (October 22, 2010), http://www.foxnews.com/us/2010/10/22/civil-rights-complaint-filed-christian-roommate-advertisement.

5. Todd Starnes, "Professor Fired over Catholic Doctrine," FOX News Radio (July 12, 2010), http://radio.foxnews.com/2010/07/12/professor-fired-over-catholic-doctrine.

6. "Pastor Says Prayer Got Him Banned from Legislative Session," WXII-TV News (July 8, 2010), http://www.wxii12.com/r/24182899/detail.html.

7. Abbe Smith, "New Haven High School Diplomas Drop Phrase 'in the Year of Our Lord,'" *New Haven Register* (June 23, 2010), http://www.nhregister.com/articles/2010/06/23/news/new_haven/aa1_nediploma062310.txt.

8. Kelli Gauthier, "National Group Demands End to Prayers at Soddy-Daisy High," *Chattanooga Times Free Press* (October 20, 2010), http://www.timesfreepress.com/news/2010/oct/20/national-group-demands-end-prayers-soddy-daisy-hig/?local.

9. Todd Starnes, "Football Prayers Banned in TN School District," ToddStarnes.com (October 20, 2010), http://toddstarnes.com/2010/10/football-prayer-under-attack-in-tennessee.

10. Janine Anderson, "Park Sophomore Finds Himself in Principal's Office after Religious 'Debate,'" *The Journal Times* (February 28, 2010), http://www.journaltimes.com/news/local/article_c9f758ae-24f0-11df-9e7f-001cc4c03286.html.

11. Sam Hodges and Kim Horner, "Dallas Housing Authority Halts Church Services at Complex for Seniors," *The Dallas Morning News* (March 4, 2010), http://www.dallasnews.com/incoming/20100303-Dallas-Housing-Authority-halts-church-services-2736.ece.

12. Todd Starnes, "Elderly Told Not to Pray Before Meals," FOX News Radio (May 10, 2010), http://radio.foxnews.com/2010/05/10/elderly-told-not-to-pray-before-meals.

13. Arek Sarkissian II, "Port Wentworth Nixes Prayer at Senior Center," *Savannah Morning News* (May 8, 2010), http://savannahnow.com/news/2010-05-08/port-wentworth-nixes-prayer-senior-center.

14. John Hinton, "Veterans Keep Vigil with the Flag," *Winston-Salem Journal* (September 24, 2010), http://www2.journalnow.com/news/2010/sep/24/they-plan-to-stay-until-rally-at-church-ar-416897.

15. "Veterans Bring Christian Flag, Plan to Stake Out Memorial," WGHP-TV (September 23, 2010), http://www.myfox8.com/news/wghp-story-group-praying-marching-100923,0,5310959.story.

16. Gerry Tuoti, "Taunton Second-Grader Sent Home over Drawing of Jesus," *Taunton Daily Gazette* (December 14, 2009), http://www.tauntongazette.com/news/x1903566059/Taunton-second-grader-suspended-over-drawing-of-Jesus.

17. Todd Starnes, "Bibles Banned in Bible Belt," FOX News Radio (January 6, 2010), http://radio.foxnews.com/2010/01/06/bibles-banned-in-bible-belt.

Chapter 31

1. Rachel Zoll, "Web Is Popular Place to 'Open' a Church", Associated Press via MSNBC News (November 1, 2009), http://www.msnbc.msn.com/id/33575348.
2. Theunis Bates, "The Twitter Bible Keeps It Short and Sacred," AOL News (August 14, 2010), http://www.aolnews.com/2010/08/14/the-twitter-bible-keeps-it-short-and-sacred.

Chapter 32

1. "Call to Action: Pastor Issuing 7-Day Sex Challenge," The Associated Press via Thestar.com (November 12, 2008), http://www.thestar.com/news/world/article/538128.

Chapter 33

1. Billy James Foote, "You Are My King," (*year unknown*).
2. Carl Gustav Boberg "How Great Thou Art," (1885).
3. Ibid.
4. George Bennard, "The Old Rugged Cross," (1912).

Chapter 34

1. "Christmas Miracle Occurs in Colorado Hospital," Associated Press via *New Haven Register* (December 30, 2009), http://www.nhregister.com/articles/2009/12/30/news/b4-notdead.txt.
2. "God Helps with Personal Decisions, Most Americans Say," *Sociology of Religion* via LiveScience.com (March 10, 2010), http://www.livescience.com/6196-god-helps-personal-decisions-americans.html.
3. Rodney Clawson, Monty Criswell, and Wade Kirby, "I Saw God Today," MCA, Nashville, (2008). Performed by George Strait.

Chapter 35

1. "Another Judicial Radical," *The Washington Times* (October 25, 2009), http://www.washingtontimes.com/news/2009/oct/25/another-judicial-radical.
2. Randy Forbes "Obama Is Wrong When He Says We're Not a Judeo-Christian Nation," *U.S. News & World Report* (May 7, 2009), http://www.usnews.com/opinion/articles/2009/05/07/obama-is-wrong-when-he-says-were-not-a-judeo-christian-nation.
3. Bill Berry, Peter Buck, Mike Mills, and Michael Stipe, "It's the End of the World as We Know It (and I Feel Fine)," produced by Scott Litt and R.E.M., I.R.S. Records (1987).